MY BROTHER'S KEEPER:
A Servant's Heart

Tariek Gahiji

WESTBOW
PRESS®
A DIVISION OF THOMAS NELSON
& ZONDERVAN

WestBow Press books may be ordered through booksellers or by contacting:

WestBow Press
A Division of Thomas Nelson & Zondervan
1663 Liberty Drive
Bloomington, IN 47403
www.westbowpress.com
844-714-3454

Unless otherwise indicated, all Scripture taken from the New King James Version®. Copyright © 1982 by Thomas Nelson. Used by permission. All rights reserved.

Scripture marked (KJV) is taken from the King James Version of the Bible.

ISBN: 978-1-6642-6083-2 (sc)
ISBN: 978-1-6642-6084-9 (hc)
ISBN: 978-1-6642-6082-5 (e)

Library of Congress Control Number: 2022904907

Print information available on the last page.

WestBow Press rev. date: 6/3/2022

Preface

"Am I my brother's keeper?" Incriminating words, indeed, as they fell from the murderous lips of Cain. As I ponder the words of Cain, I ask myself, are we any less guilty when it comes to regarding the welfare of others? Do we try to conceal our neglect to respond to the needs of others, as Cain tried to conceal his disregard for the life of his brother, Abel? Do we say that he's not my responsibility, or pretend that we didn't know their situation, as Cain did? Because that's what he was doing when he said to God, "I know not. Am I my brother's keeper?" Do we tell ourselves that we can't help everyone, when we really aren't giving our all to anyone, to soothe our conscience?

Yes, some of us may say we give to charities. We give to those in need whenever we can. We give whatever we can to the homeless. But I'm not talking about our occasional donations we give out of convenience. I'm not talking about the numerous token gifts we may give to avoid getting involved in that person's life. No, I'm talking about us giving of ourselves to those in need with a commitment to helping them maintain a sense of stability, dignity, and hope in their lives until they can provide for themselves.

I'm not just talking about monetary needs. I'm talking about committing ourselves to one another's needs whatever the need may be, in whatever capacity we may be able to give. Money may not be the issue. There may be a need for our presence and comfort during a trying time in someone's life. Or there may be a need for counseling and guidance in areas that we qualify in helping them work out their problems. There are so many ways that we can be "helpers one to the other" that do not always involve giving money but simply giving of ourselves.

It is my prayer that God uses me to help us develop a better understanding in our responsibility for one another within the Body of Christ, as well as to our fellowman. I remember a pastor saying that the church's purpose was not to operate as an institution to answer all the social ills of today, for that was the government's responsibility. I agree with his statement to a degree. The church as an organization is not responsible, nor structured, to remedy every need of society. But as the Body of Christ, I believe we as members can pool our interests and resources together to make a difference in the lives of others, especially in the lives of our fellow brothers and sisters in Christ.

We may not see it this way, but we are dependent upon one another regardless of our abundant or limited resources. Dependent upon God without a doubt;

however, God also purposely created us as relational creatures with a common bond to one another. As the saying goes, "No man is an island." We may as well realize as one of us falls, so does the whole of man eventually. All we must do is look around to witness this tragedy in progress. The wealth of a few is steadily increasing at the expense of many. I don't believe God intended it to be that way. The sin of humans ushered in the many practices that are tearing away at our sense of affinity with one another.

We're all created by God, made from the same substance—the dust of the earth—received the same breath of life, and every one of us became a living soul (Genesis 2:7). Sadly, we don't all think in common, and that's where most of our difficulties arise when it comes to gravitating toward one another's needs. Our sinful nature will not allow us to prefer each other's welfare over our own. However, as people of God, we are to be led by the Holy Spirit and have an interest in addressing the needs of those within as well as outside the Body of Christ.

Some of you can pick up your jaw now, because incredulous as it may sound, I not only believe that it is possible but that it is scripture based as well. Are we fulfilling the will of God by caring for one another's needs? Do we have a genuine interest in each other's welfare, and if so, are we using what's available to us to benefit those in need? Always keeping in mind that needs come in many different forms and are not limited to a monetary one, but our contribution to each other's needs could be done through channels other than financial ones. One thing is for certain—it's going to cost us something. It may cost us some time, inconvenience, discomfort, and even sacrifice. But whatever the cost, it will be well worth it knowing that we are being helpers one to another as God intended.

1

THAT'S NOT WHAT GOD INTENDED

*Then God blessed them, and God said
to them, "Be fruitful and multiply;
fill the earth and subdue it."*

(GENESIS 1:28 NKJV)

It was always God's intention for man to have dominion over His creations in the earth, and for Him to have dominion over the soul of man. However, when sin entered in by human disobedience to God's will, things changed drastically. Those changes have been ongoing since humankind's fall from God's grace. The way God originally structured things to be for humans was not altered by God but through human disobedience.

When God gave His commandment to be fruitful and multiply, He not only meant for humans to procreate, but for humans and His other creations to be productive and bear fruit as well. Not sparingly, but in great abundance. God purposed for humans to work: "Then the Lord God took the man and put him in the Garden of Eden to tend and keep it" (Genesis 2:15 NKJV). Not as we view work today, but as being a part of our nature in reverence to God. It wasn't until after our fall from God's grace that our laboring became a hardship:

> Then to Adam he said, Because you have heeded the voice of your wife, and have eaten from the tree of which I commanded you, saying, you shall not eat of it: Cursed is the ground for your sake; In toil you shall eat of it all the days of your life. Both thorns and thistles it shall bring forth for you, and you shall eat the herb of the field. In the sweat of your face you shall eat bread till you return to the ground, for out of it you were taken; for dust you are, and to dust you shall return. (Genesis 3 :17–19 NKJV)

Things changed for us when sin was ushered in through the disobedience of one human. And there's no need of us blaming Adam because we all would have done the same: "Therefore, just as through one man sin entered the world, and death through sin, and thus death spread to all men, because all have sinned" (Romans 5.12 NKJV).

We now must labor for a living. Even those who live what we consider comfortable lives must labor, if for no other reason than dealing with the mental stress of holding onto what they believe to be theirs, which could become more taxing on one's health than physical labor. Laboring more and more for material gain and not realizing the thin line between possessing what they have and losing it. Ask the rich man who thought he had it all before death came knocking at his door (Luke 12:16–21). We can make the same mistake the rich man made by thinking that the things we have are ours to do with however we see fit. Yet the truth of the matter is that hoarding our possessions only results in our spiritual detriment toward God, because we hinder God's blessings for us when we neglect to share them with others.

The Way of the World

Let's get one thing clear; the world as a whole does not care about the welfare of others to the point of sharing out of an act of kinship. Oddly enough, you would think that those who are less fortunate would tend to express a greater understanding for those in similar situations, but that is not always the case. Having a little does not mean that we will not hold onto what we have just as tightly, if not tighter than those who are wealthy. Our way of thinking just isn't geared toward giving away the things we believe to be ours, especially if we had to work hard for them. Why should we share our things with someone who had nothing to do with helping us get to where we are? Let them work just as hard as we did and earn their keep; no free rides here, my friend.

We see the need for greed more prominent today than ever. You now have megacorporations basing their profits on how much they surpassed their previous quarter. Being in the black is no longer the gauge in determining a company's success but rather how much more can they exceed last year's profits.

There's nothing wrong with trying to increase profits; that's the main reason for establishing a business—to make money. However, when increased profits take priority over people's lives, disaster is soon to follow. You can see it all around you; conglomerates (megacorporations) downsize out of an appeal to decrease their losses, when what they're really doing is trying to increase their profits by any means necessary. If that means destroying lives in the process, so be it.

I understand that some companies need to increase their profits to stay in business, but you are beginning to see more companies gearing their motives toward purely maximizing their profits not out of need but greed. A $100 million profit last year was great, so a $200 million profit is the goal for this year. Now here's the kicker, if they fall short of that goal, or God forbid they should make less than they did last year, even though the monies made resulted in profits sufficient to sustain the company, it's considered a loss. Fifty million dollars profit is not acceptable, the agenda is to make more and more and more, at all cost.

Do I have documented proof of this type of practice? No, but I ask you, how is it that major corporations can file bankruptcy one day and dissolve their company completely, wiping out thousands of jobs and pensions, and be allowed to start another business under a different corporate title and still be solvent? I'll tell you how; they were never really in financial trouble. They just ran out of ways to increase their profits, so their last option was to dissolve the company so they could start anew with scaled-down pay, limited or no health care, no unions—whatever it takes to cut costs, even though the cost doesn't jeopardize survival of the company.

So, what's the motive behind this continual progression of increasing profits if not to keep the company solvent? I personally believe to increase one's worth to compete in that arena called "Power and Control." I'm certain this is not the only reason, but I would say that it's a large percentage of it. Think about it, how many thousands, millions, or billions does a person need to live comfortably? It gets to a point where one's wealth becomes obscene in relation to the needs, as well as rights of others.

Some of you may be curious as to the spiritual content of what I'm talking about. Just bear with me; I'm getting there. When I say needs and rights of others, I'm referring to what I believe is every man's God-given right. I believe God purposed for everyone to be productive making their own provisions. Let's look at Genesis 1:28 again and try to connect God's commandment to Adam to our present-day situation. This verse states a lot because it's God's directive to man regarding his role and purpose. It's mentioned two times in the Bible where it is given directly to man from God; one time to Adam and Eve, and another time to Noah and his sons (Genesis 9:1–2). These are two key occurrences because both involve a beginning, one after God's creation of Adam and Eve, and the other after God's judgment upon His creation.

Be fruitful and multiply is used by God to all His creation, man (Genesis 1:28; 9:1–2) and creature (Genesis 1:22; 8:17). But note when God speaks to man, He also includes "replenish the earth," and informs him of his dominion over His other creations on earth. When I looked up the Hebrew definition for replenish, the root word, *mala*, meant: to fill, or be full of, in a wide application (literally and figuratively). From this it seems that God is not only telling humans to be productive and bear fruit in abundance, but in such a way as to fill the earth, and as humans and God's other creations fill the earth, humans will have dominion.

Considering this, it only seems logical that God giving such a directive would also make provisions for humanity to sustain itself. God does not leave us to our logic but lets us know his intentions and purpose for humans and his other creations: "And God said, see, I have given you every herb that yields seed which is on the face of all the earth, and every tree whose fruit yields seed; to you it shall be for food. Also, to every beast of the earth, to every bird of the air, and to everything that creeps on the earth, in which there is life, I have given every green herb for food: and it was so" (Genesis 1:29–30 NKJV). God tells Adam and Eve that He has made provisions for all His creation, and as they procreate (reproduce/increase), so will the provisions of God. These provisions are available to all, because it is a God-given right, ordained by God.

God intended for all His creation's *needs* to be met (emphasis on needs), but as with most things, when sin entered in, so did the depravity of humanity. God never intended for us to be in a deprived state, but God understood that with humans' fall also came their corruption. Human corruption does not allow people to regard the welfare of others. Yes, we have those who can be credited with altruistic acts of one kind or another, but as a whole, the world's mind-set is not to succeed for the benefit of others but for their own personal gain and accumulation of wealth.

You'd be hard-pressed to find someone who has not at one time or another contemplated being rich. It's something that's hard to avoid, especially in a capitalistic society. The great American dream is no longer to own a home but to become rich as quickly as possible. How do you think casinos, lotteries, scam artists, racetracks, and any other institutions meant to milk people's money for their personal gain exist? By continually waving in front of us the desire that many have, and that is to become wealthy. Human nature overcomes us just as Israel's nature did in the wilderness when God provided them with quail and manna from heaven. Instead of gathering enough for their daily consumption and disposing of the remains before morning as instructed, they kept it, and it spoiled with worms and caused a stench throughout the camp (Exodus 16:10–21).

Greedy humans would rather hoard their resources before sharing it with those in need. Think I'm wrong? Go behind some of the ritzy hotels you know of and rummage through some of their garbage, if you dare to, and see how much food they throw away every day. I'm talking about food that's not spoiled or ruined. You'd be amazed at the amount of food that goes to waste. But let some homeless person ask for it, and no, they would rather throw it away than to give it to someone in need. I know someone is saying that there could be legal ramifications for them doing so. With the lawsuit frenzy that's going on these days, I can consider that, but more often than not, that's usually a smoke screen used to relieve them of any accountability to their indifference to people in need.

I witnessed a situation where a company I once worked for produced certain food products and refused to donate items that had reached their expiration dates to a food depository that was directly across the street from them. There was no danger of legal repercussions because I personally found out that certain foods could still be consumed after their expiration date; they just could not be sold, and the foods that they produced fell in that category. The problem was that they just didn't care enough to concern themselves with other people's needs.

Now when you consider humanity's fallen nature, and then add materialism to it, you will inevitably end up with greed. We all desire material things for our lives; the question is, how much? Have some of our desires become lusts? Have we developed an uncontrolled willingness to do about anything for material gain? That's how the world operates, and that is why we will always have a disparity between the haves and the have-nots. So, what are we to do? Break away from the stigma of materialism (greed) and learn to operate according to God's will. It will not rid the world of all its social inequities, but it will make a world of difference within the Body of Christ.

God's People

It's up to God's people to govern their lives as God intended, and that is to bear their fruits to replenish the earth. Not as the world does by hoarding all of it for their own personal gain, but by sharing it with others, and that must begin within the Body of Christ. Sadly, the stench that arises from greed is taking more of a foothold in the lives of God's people than we care to admit, and that shouldn't be.

Now I'm not saying God does not desire for us to enjoy the bounties of life. Throughout the Bible there are documentations of God's people living affluent lives, and so can we. The key is do we have the same spirit as they did in sharing their wealth? I know that some weren't as giving as others, just as we have today, but I'm not talking about them. I'm talking about those Old Testament as well as New Testament saints who had a heart for God in sharing their wealth. I plan to discuss a few of the instances where it shows that they did not keep their wealth just for themselves but purposely shared it with others.

Throughout the Bible are documented instances where the wealth of God's people benefited the body of those within their care as a whole. Let me try to explain what I mean by within their care. Take Abraham, for example. After leaving his family and land, God blessed him greatly, and with those blessings came great wealth for him and his family (Genesis 13:2, 5–6). Now I don't recall, maybe some of you will, that when Abraham prospered, any of his family, servants, handmaidens, or anyone else who was within his care was ever in need. Why? Because Abraham, having a heart for God, understood that his wealth was not just for himself or his immediate family but for those within his care as well. In other words, those who were in reach of Abraham benefited from Abraham.

Abraham was willing to meet the needs of others, not out of obligation, but probably out of a sense of accountability to God in being a faithful steward in managing the wealth God blessed him with to benefit others. The heart that Abraham had for God did not allow him to turn a blind eye to the needs of others, and that's the message I believe God has inspired me to convey to His people. I plan to go into greater detail as to how I believe God expects us to give for the sake of others. But right now, I'm just trying to get us to understand that we should not be functioning as the world does.

I'm not trying to advocate that we can totally cure the world of poverty, because that's not possible due to the sinfulness of man. It's not from any insensitivity or inability of God that He does not destroy the conditions of the poor resulting from sin, but it's his mercy for the souls of those who remain to receive salvation. Sin is the catalyst to the evils of the world (humans), and for God to destroy the probability of sin's consequences He would have to destroy sin itself. Now if God were to destroy sin right now, a lot of souls would be lost that are ordained by God to be saved. And God is not going to do that just to appease the cries of humans, even for those who are His. Sin is the result of human disobedience to God's will, and we must deal with the consequences of sin until God completes the work He purposed to accomplish through our Lord and Savior Jesus Christ, which is to save the souls that have been predestined for Himself (Ephesians 1:3–5).

The consequences of sin will not be destroyed until

sin itself is destroyed, along with the father of it—Satan. However, that doesn't negate the things we can do to help ease the effects that he has had on people's lives. Throughout this book as I refer to "lives," I'm talking about a certain quality of life that everyone needs to function as productive human beings. As I said before, there are certain God-given rights God made provisions for that were intended for every human, but with human sin also came an altering process of human nature that tips the original scales of God's intended parity of humans.

Now with man's nature, there's no hope of tipping these scales back in the direction of God, but with His people there is, because we now have the Spirit of God to guide us. In the Old Testament, you'll witness that those who lived righteously before God, when they prospered, so did God's people, as well as those who were blessed to be associated with them. Joseph is a prime example of this happening. He went through a lot before reaching a position of prominence, but when God finally positioned him, his favors of God blessed Egypt as well as Israel. Read the account for yourself (Genesis chapters 41–45:1–8).

There are two verses I would like to briefly mention from the scriptures I just gave you (Genesis 45:5, 7 NKJV): "But now, do not therefore be grieved or angry with yourselves because you sold me here: for God sent me before you to preserve life … And God sent me before you to preserve a posterity for you in the earth, and to save your lives by a great deliverance." Check out Joseph; after all he's been through knowing that his brothers are the ones who sold him into slavery, rather than focus on the injustices that were committed against him and the things he suffered, he centered his attention on the purposes of God. He accepted with joy God using him to preserve life, and to save not only the lives of his brothers but to preserve the future generations of Israel.

Now what am I getting at? Well, I'm wondering how many of us are willing to consider and dare to believe that when God blesses His children with an abundance of resources, He's doing so with the intention of using some of those resources to also improve the quality of life for those within the Body of Christ; as well as those who God may place in our path with a need we can fill. No one can do it all, nor does God expect us to. But I do believe that God desires for those who are blessed with wealth to put forth a concerted and unified effort to use their wealth to address the needs of others, especially those within the Body Christ.

I say especially within the Body of Christ because it must first begin with God's people. As they say, charity must first begin at home before you can help anyone else. No father can expect God to bless him serving everyone else's needs before providing for his own family. He must first meet the needs of those for whom God has given him responsibility, before receiving the blessings of God to help others. Too often we find many of us who have the resources to help others, and are doing so, but oftentimes at the expense of our fellow brothers and sisters in Christ. We're stepping over people who are desperate for help with no regard of our responsibility for their needs as members of God's family: "Therefore as we have opportunity, let us do good to all, especially to those who are of the household of faith" (Galatians 6:10 NKJV).

As God's people, we have a responsibility to exercise ourselves as faithful stewards with God's blessings and not treat them as our own personal property. When we hoard our possessions, we're no different than the world and may be guilty of gaining our riches as the world does: "As a partridge broods but does not hatch, so is he who gets riches, but not by right; it will leave him in the midst of his days, and at his end he will be a fool" (Jeremiah 17:11 NKJV). You will find few who have gained their wealth unjustly willing to share it with others freely, because they have a thief's heart that doesn't believe in giving. It takes those who have a heart for God to understand that the only gains that will flourish are those obtained through God. When that occurs, it should only come naturally to share our surplus, because we no longer view our possessions as ours, but God's.

No Other Way

Human ambitions have resulted in a severe shortage in their makeup. It's not common for us to have a genuine compassion for others in general. Every aspect of man has been tainted to some degree, whether it involves our talents (special abilities we may possess), our time (something many of us are reluctant to sacrifice for others), or our possessions (money, home, clothes, food, anything of a material nature that we could share). It's not our nature to give of ourselves with the welfare of others in mind. Sadder is that, even though many of us may not be endowed as richly in certain areas of our lives as others, we fail to realize that we still have something to offer that God can use to enrich the life of someone else. Contributing to a person's life isn't always dependent upon monetary means.

When God told Abraham to leave his country and family, God not only said that He would bless Abraham but that Abraham would be a blessing, "I will make you a great nation; I will bless you and make your name great; and you shall be a blessing. I will bless those who bless you, and I will curse him who curses you; and in you all the families of the earth shall be blessed" (Genesis 12:2–3 NKJV). This promise that God made to Abraham has a blanket effect for all of mankind. God tells Abraham He's going to bless him, and from that he will be a blessing. He's going to bless them that bless Abraham, and curse them that curse him, and through Abraham all families of the earth shall be blessed. From such a promise it is hard not to see that God purposed to bless others through His chosen people. God chose

Abraham to covenant with, not Abraham with God. And with that covenant, God immediately lets Abraham know that the blessings from His covenant with him will serve to benefit humans collectively.

Abraham, and the nation of Israel that God promised, is also a type for us to learn from. God chose Abraham to become the father of many, and that was not exclusive to Israel (Galatians 3:7). Israel became God's chosen people through Abraham, not out of any greatness or goodness of their own, but because God promised it to be so with Abraham and purposed to use Israel as His vessel to bless other nations. Israel failed miserably in realizing God's purpose, but it never changed God's plan.

Israel's pride in themselves being God's chosen blinded them to the greater good of being used by God to benefit their fellowman. So much so that their pride became so deep rooted that many of them failed to see the revelation of Jesus Christ as Savior, and still do, believing that only Judaism qualified one to become a member of God's family (Acts 15:1–5). It may seem that I'm veering from the subject at hand, but I'm not, because just as Israel failed to see God's purpose in them to be a blessing for other nations, we as God's people today are failing miserably in realizing our position in Christ of fulfilling the promise given to Abraham in being a blessing to the families of the earth. Will everyone benefit? No. But we should fashion our lives in such a way that we will affect the lives of many with the things we have to offer, instead of being fearful of losing them.

Without a doubt many of us are fulfilling the role we all have been called out for in touching the lives of many for God to draw unto salvation. But we are failing miserably in dealing with the total makeup of humanity and their needs. The most important thing that can happen in anyone's life is his or her spiritual rebirth (salvation) in Jesus Christ. However, for us to stop there and leave everything else unattended when we can give so much more is irresponsible to the call of God for us to care for one another. How we relate to one another within the Body of Christ is crucial to how we affect the lives of those outside the Body of Christ. Until we learn how to care for each other within the Body of Christ, we will never fully experience the difference that God can make with our lives in the world.

It's through us that God plans on changing the lives of many, not just spiritually but naturally as well. Jesus Christ during His earthly ministry addressed the natural condition of humankind along with their spiritual, even though the spiritual need was of greater importance. Many times, Jesus would address their natural needs before even revealing anything of a spiritual nature to them. Why would Jesus make such an approach knowing that a human's spiritual state with God far outweighs his or her natural needs when it comes to salvation? Well, I believe that Jesus understands that people's natural needs can cloud their need for anything else if not dealt with appropriately. Wonder why so many people leave the church after receiving salvation? The answer in part could be out of our indifference to their needs.

We see people without food, without decent clothes to wear, depressed from losing their job, grieving over a lost loved one, in need of counsel and assistance to deal with a troubled child or marriage. We see, we see, we see. And they know we are aware of their situation because they have shared it with us. And what do we do? Too often we resort to that old faithful adage, "If you need anything just let me know; I'm here for you," when what we are really saying is, "I'm here for you, but I hope that you don't ask me for anything, because I really don't want to get involved with your problems if it's going to require more than I'm willing to give," which isn't much. We like to hear ourselves talk. It makes us feel good. When in reality all we plan on doing is giving them something as quickly and conveniently as possible and hope we can disappear from their "go to saint list" as soon as possible. We even go as far as trying to steer them away from ourselves to someone else in hopes of relieving ourselves of the responsibility.

We can look around all we want to, but the bottom line is that God has chosen His people as His channel to rebuild the lives that sin is destroying. I've said it before and will be saying it as often as need be. God intended for every human to be productive. God desires for all His creation to contribute in some way or another. Lives are being destroyed every day as people continue to fall through the cracks of society's ills not because they are irresponsible and lazy, but due to the consequences of sin. For centuries now, the greed of a few has caused the grief of many. And as the tentacles of capitalism continue to reach throughout the world, the quality of life for many is being lost.

The direction of the world today seems to be "every man for himself." Individualism is the way to go. The more I increase myself through possessions, the more power and control I have. It's not for me to improve the lives of others but to step on and over them. After all, if I were to help rebuild their lives, they might destroy mine. I can't allow anyone to gain the upper hand against me, so it's not wise for me to share what I have with those who will benefit from it. I can control things better when I can keep them in a needful state, yeah, that's the way to go.

What's the big deal anyway? People are more expendable these days. They come and go. I don't need them; they need me. What do they have to offer me for what I can do for them? Am I supposed to just help them because they're in need? No one did that for me. Maybe it's true that some of their conditions result from the injustices of a materialistic, power-driven, self-centered world. What does that have to do with me? I'm just trying to make it like anyone else. And the justification conversation goes on and on as far as the world is concerned, but it must stop when it comes to God's people. God has a different plan for our lives, and a different method by which we are to operate in relation to each other's needs.

It must begin with the Body of Christ if there is to be any hope at all of restoring lives. We must stop excusing ourselves from helping people under the cloak of depending upon God to make the difference. There is no doubt that it can only be done through God, but we keep running from His method, which is to use the lives of His people to fulfill His purpose. God's people, not the world, because the world does not have the heart of God; we do. So, if anyone is going to set an example of brotherly love with a communal environment, it's going to be done by the hand of God through God's people. When God blesses us, we should bless other people's lives as well. Beginning first with the Body of Christ and then throughout the world. It is my prayer that God speaks to the hearts of His people and reveals to them through His word that there is a call on our lives to fill the void that sin created between man being his "brother's keeper," understanding that this care must first begin within the Body of Christ before it can reach those outside of it.

2

PROSPERITY

Beloved, I pray that you may prosper
in all things and be in health,
just as your soul prospers.

(3 JOHN 2 NKJV)

Prosperity is something that God desires for all His children and yet is something that many of us may never experience. How can this be when it is designed in God's will for us to live prosperous lives? Other than the most obvious reason we can think of—failing to live upright lives before God—is there something else that hinders us from enjoying the prosperity that apostle John speaks of in 3 John 2? I believe there is, and it hinges upon our interpretation of what we consider to be prosperity according to God.

For many, prosperity is defined by how much one has acquired. A nice income, beautiful homes, luxury cars, stylish clothes, substantial investments, and all the other frills that are considered gauges for success. However, as we study the word of God and learn more about His will for us, can we honestly believe that God measures our prosperity by our material wealth? Are we so shortsighted that we fail to see the richness in Jesus's life during His earthly ministry that overshadows material gain?

I'm not suggesting that our prosperity in God is determined by our lack of material things, for I do not believe that we must be impoverished in order to be prosperous in God. What I am saying is that we need to reevaluate our perspective of what we consider to be prosperity so that we can make certain that it parallels with God's will. When we consider how all of creation originates from God and is entirely dependent upon Him for its continued existence, material gain is but a small thing for God to grant us. We cannot afford to allow ourselves to become deceived by the world's customary standards of measuring prosperity. Our Father is greater than the material things He has created for us, and it is only through understanding God's meaning of prosperity that we are able to truly enjoy and benefit from material wealth.

Prosperity in God

To begin to experience the prosperity that provides a godly balance for our lives, we must first understand prosperity as God revealed it to apostle John. In 3 John

2, John speaks of prosperity, and he expresses his desire for Gaius's prosperity to abound in three areas: in general, in health, and in his soul. What seems to be John's focus is that Gaius's prosperity be based upon how well his soul prospers. Notice how John ends the verse with "just as your soul prospers" (or to say, just as your soul prospers, or the same as your soul prospers). I looked up the words *prosper* and *soul*, and according to *The New Strong's Exhaustive Concordance*, the Greek term for prosper (*euodoo*) means to help on the road (i.e., (passively) succeed in reaching; figuratively, to succeed in business affairs). In other words, that they have a prosperous journey. And the Greek term for soul (*psuche*) means breath (i.e., breath of life, spirit, abstract or concrete). Keep in mind the spirit that is being spoken of in reference to the soul is the spirit of life that God originally breathed into man, making him a living soul (Genesis 2:7). I also looked up the word *passive*, and the definitions I believe to be most fitting from *Webster's Collegiate Dictionary* is: (1) acted upon by an external agency, and (2) receptive to outside impressions or influences. For the sake of clarity, I would like to replace the words *external* and *outside* for these definitions with *internal* since the influence we are to operate from originates with God's Spirit that dwells within those of us who belong to Christ.

Considering the information before us, I believe the message John is conveying to God's people as he writes to Gaius is that his hope is for God's people to enjoy a good life. A life that is full of achievements and good health, not from any power of our own, but from the spiritual riches of God's Spirit permeating our very souls. It is the spiritual growth within our soul that John is more concerned with, than with our material gains in the world. Placed in the proper context according to the meanings that are given us, along with the verses that follow (3 John 3–8), it is extremely difficult, if not impossible, to conclude that John's interpretation of prosperity is based upon our material wealth versus our spiritual richness in God. No, John makes it very clear that the spiritual growth within our soul is of much greater importance and that if we are to prosper in anything, it must first be within our soul.

Immediately after expressing his hope for Gaius's prosperity, John reveals what he has joy in the most— that they are living according to God's word (3 John 3–4). Not how successful they have become in worldly gains, but how well they are prospering in living their lives for Christ. God, through John, purposely did this, I believe, so that we would not confuse material riches with the prosperity that God desires for us. God will not allow earthly wealth to obscure the spiritual riches that can only be gained through the knowledge of His word. God knows that a life void of the knowledge of Jesus Christ is empty regardless of accomplishments. It is a life that will be dysfunctional at best because it will lack the guidance of God's Spirit.

John ties in living godly lives with being faithful

toward our brothers and sisters in Christ, as well as our fellow man (3 John 5). This faithfulness that we show toward others expresses our faithfulness to God and testifies of our love throughout the Body of Christ. Not some misguided and aimless faithfulness, but one that has direction—one that has purpose. John reveals what our focus and purpose should be, which is to use the love of God within us to guide others into living godly lives (3 John 6). And living godly lives is closely knitted to how well we relate to one another, how we reach out to each other and how willing we are to extend goodwill toward our brothers and sisters in Christ, as well as those outside the Body of Christ.

True prosperity arises from our efforts to extend ourselves to help others. For by doing so we express the heart of Jesus. Jesus Christ came as a direct expression of His love for us and our needs (Luke 4:18), embodying the heart of God. It was the heart of God within Jesus Christ that directed Jesus's heart toward God, and thereby the riches of God flowed through Jesus Christ unto us. Jesus's desire is not only for our salvation, but to also share His riches with us as brethren. Jesus Christ did not come to withhold things from us; no, He set aside His royalty to be our Savior that He would be able to share His wealth with us. Jesus Christ did not come to pursue riches, but to share them. Jesus had no need to pursue the things that were already His. The point is that He was willing to give them up to become our Savior (Hebrews 2:9–11). Jesus Christ surrendered His riches to enrich our lives—for our benefit, for our increase, for our welfare. Jesus Christ's Spirit was rich in His Father, and rich toward us. When Jesus came as our Savior, He did not come preferring Himself. He came preferring the will of God, which is the redemption of our souls. His death on the cross testifies to that. And Jesus's continued care for us now exemplifies His desire to make provisions for our every need.

What's important is whether we are exemplifying prosperity through the eyes of Jesus Christ or as the world views it. Through Jesus's vision, we'll be rich toward God, those within the Body of Christ, as well as our fellow man. However, from a worldly outlook, we would find it extremely difficult to practice the genuine richness of Jesus's Spirit toward God, much less toward anyone else. How we relate to one another is in direct proportion to how much we are connected to the heart of Jesus Christ. Our richness toward others expresses our richness toward God.

Prosperity in Others

I personally believe that teachers hold one of the most significant positions for human development. From our infancy to our childhood, adolescence, and adulthood, we have directly or indirectly been influenced by someone else's teachings and beliefs. Whether their influence was of a positive or negative nature didn't matter; what mattered was the amount of time we were exposed to their influences. Those who were willing to invest more time into our lives were those who more likely would have an influence upon the direction our lives would take. Of course, there are other factors to consider when determining one's makeup, like cultural practices and environment. But whatever factors we may consider, how we interpret them is usually influenced by the teachings to which we're exposed.

Teachers come from all walks of life—the most common one being as a vocation within our multilevel school systems—and yet there are so many other channels by which we learn. Parents, relatives, neighbors, friends, peer groups, pastors, church leaders, the list is vast. The point I'm trying to make is that teachers come in all shapes and forms. And what makes them stand out more than anything is the common thread that a committed teacher exhibits, which is a genuine desire to invest their educational resources into people's lives for their enrichment.

Teachers are fascinating and unique people, because those who have a sincere desire to teach are not just driven out of a choice of vocation, but out of a passion for it. Their interests run much deeper than just earning an income. They don't need a classroom full of students to prompt them to teach; it's something they do daily inside the classroom as well as out. Their interest in the lives of those they teach causes them to invest themselves into their lives with a hope of impacting them for a lifetime.

Now what does that have to do with "prosperity in others," you might ask? Well, just as devoted teachers have a sincere desire to invest themselves into the lives of those they teach, so should God's people have a sincere desire to invest their lives into the lives of others. There are very few things more rewarding than investing oneself into someone else's life purely out of a zeal and passion for their well-being. And for this passion to have a genuine and lasting value, it must stem from God's love.

Jesus Christ personally invested Himself into twelve individuals, whom we know as His apostles, and through them began a turn of events that could have never been accomplished if Jesus had withheld the riches of His glory from their lives. Through those twelve, Jesus began the promise that God made to Israel and mankind:

> Behold, the days are coming, says the LORD, when I will make a new covenant with the house of Israel and with the house of Judah; not according to the covenant that I made with their fathers in the day that I took them by the hand to lead them out of the land of Egypt, My covenant which they broke, though I was a husband to them, says the LORD: But this is the covenant that I will make with the house of Israel

after those days, says the LORD: I will put My law in their minds, and write it on their hearts; and I will be their God, and they shall be My people. No more shall every man teach his neighbor, and every man his brother, saying, "Know the LORD," for they shall all know Me, from the least of them to the greatest of them, says the LORD. For I will forgive their iniquity, and their sin I will remember no more. (Jeremiah 31:31–34 NKJV).

To avoid any misunderstanding with verse 34, please don't go running off thinking that now that we have received the spiritual adoption that God has promised us, that we have all become self-teachers of the deeper principles of God's word and no longer have a need for God's teachers (Ephesians 4:11–13), because that is not what's being said. No, rather than us remaining in darkness, our hearts being oblivious to God, we now have within us the nature (His Holy Spirit) to know and to receive the things of God. We are no longer strangers but God's children, and kinsmen with Jesus Christ, who are still in need of instruction from those who God has ordained for that purpose.

Not to veer off course, let me get back to the subject of us investing in one another. Very few things are more rewarding than depositing oneself into the life of another. Money can't buy the spiritual riches one gains for their soul's enrichment when giving unconditionally to another for their welfare. That's what Jesus did for us. He gave Himself unconditionally for our benefit. And not just for a moment but for a lifetime that spans throughout time and into eternity. Jesus's prosperity was in doing the will of His Father, and that will was for Jesus to make an investment for the salvation of our souls. And in that salvation, Jesus continues to give according to our needs to increase us spiritually and naturally. God understands that we have natural needs. The question seems to be as representatives of Christ, do we understand the balance between spiritual and natural as we relate to one another? "If a brother or sister is naked and destitute of daily food, and one of you says to them, 'Depart in peace, be warmed and filled,' but you do not give them the things which are needed for the body, what does it profit?" (James 2:15–16 NKJV).

I find it hard to imagine us contributing to the lives of others while we step over and upon those we are spiritually connected to within the Body of Christ. Where's the prosperity in neglecting the needs of those who are our brothers and sisters in Christ? Charity must first begin within the Body of Christ before we are able to prosper outside of it. Please understand that the kind of prosperity in others I believe God desires for me to convey is one that is ongoing throughout our sanctified lives. One that doesn't end until the day we die, for to prosper means to flourish.

Flowers are known to flourish in their beauty

when they bloom in the rays of God's sunshine. This is something they do continually if they have life in their roots. It's not until they lose that life that they fail to flourish and bloom according to their given nature. We as God's people have the nature of Jesus Christ, but sad to say are not living according to the nature that is within us. Our spirit is alive with the Spirit of God dwelling within; however, the roots in some of our souls are dead and fail to operate from the power of the Spirit of Christ. It's not something that God desires, but it's very real just the same. We're not spiritually dead; we're just too much into ourselves for our souls to respond to the spiritual urgings that our spirit is receiving from God.

How sad. The reality of this is that we will never be able to fulfill a life of prospering in others until we put forth an active effort to first yield to the Spirit of Jesus Christ. It's not something that's just going to happen without our putting forth a conscious effort to exercise the nature of God's Spirit that dwells within us daily. Our prosperity in others is not measured by how much we give for the moment but by how much we are willing to give of ourselves for as long and as often as needed, within our ability to do so. God is not asking us to neglect nor put ourselves or our families in the poor house. However, we need to stop hiding behind the pretense that we are doing our part, when we know that we would do a whole lot more if we were committed to others as much as we would desire them to be to us in our time of need.

Earthly Riches Are Deceiving

The success of a person's life from the world's perspective is often determined by how much wealth has been accumulated. For God's people, this can be a very misleading and detrimental practice. Just because a person happens to be privileged enough to enjoy a lot of the benefits that come along with being wealthy does not mean that they are people of integrity. Their wealth does not signify that they are governed by high moral standards. The same can apply to God's people as well; their wealth and seemingly boundless blessings do not necessarily mean that they are in good standing with God.

Too often we place value in the wrong things for determining our favor with God. The truth of the matter is that we can be just as ruthless and uncaring as some secular people when accumulating wealth. Our material prosperity should be the last thing we use for gauging our spiritual richness in God. Look how God viewed Israel during their time of abundance and lavish living:

> But this people has a defiant and a rebellious heart; they have revolted and departed. They do not say in their heart,

Let us now fear the LORD our God, Who gives rain, both the former and the latter, in its season. He reserves for us the appointed weeks of the harvest. Your iniquities have turned these things away, and your sins have withheld good from you. For among my people are found wicked men: they lie wait as one who set snares; they set a trap; they catch men. As a cage is full of birds, so their houses are full of deceit. Therefore they have become great and grown rich. They have grown fat, they are sleek; yes, they surpass the deeds of the wicked; they do not plead the cause, the cause of the fatherless; yet they prosper, and the right of the needy they do not defend. Shall I not punish them for these things? says the LORD. Shall I not avenge Myself on such a nation as this? An astonishing and horrible thing has been committed in the land: The prophets prophesy falsely, and the priests rule by their own power: and my people love to have it so. But what will you do in the end? (Jeremiah 5:23–31 NKJV)

To state it bluntly, Israel had become corrupt and wicked people in their time of abundance.

Let's take a closer look at a few of these verses from Jeremiah, and see if we can relate to them for today. We can begin with verses 26 and 27; look how God indicts them of being wicked and evil people. Why? They have resorted to underhanded and deceitful ways for advancing themselves. I remember having a discussion with a brother in Christ, who has his own business, about how seemingly in this era, megabusinesses no longer determine their profits by a profit-and-loss system, but by how much more they can increase their profits from last year's gains. The response I got from him surprised me somewhat, but I understood how he could say what he did. His response was that businesses had to increase their profits, even at the expense of jeopardizing the livelihood of others, to stay competitive and survive.

We continued with our discussion for about twenty minutes or so, until I realized that we were on different frequencies. One frequency tuned in to gaining success by secular standards, and the other frequency tuned in to succeeding with God and people's welfare in mind. The way my precious brother continued to defend what I thought was obviously unscrupulous downsizing techniques used by so many of the companies today, purely out of a need for greed, told me that he had missed my point totally. What I was trying to get him to see is that God's people should not operate according to world standards. There's no doubt in my mind that people can be successful without compromising God's boundaries of integrity.

Without God's intervention, whatever we may accomplish is unstable at best. And more than likely has been tainted by some form of selfish means to get it and keep it. We need to understand that God does not gauge sin by degrees. What we may consider a minor foul, or just a way of doing business to survive, is corruption to God. There's no sin in acquiring wealth or being well-off. However, how we obtain and keep that wealth, as well as how we use it, is of great significance in the sight of God. We say we have faith, and trust in God, so why don't we trust Him to preserve our business as we operate according to His standards, for His glory? Some of us may not agree, but with wealth comes great responsibility. There's more accountability for those who God blesses with His wealth. We shouldn't accumulate and hoard wealth the way the world does. It only clogs our spiritual arteries, blocking the lifeline to our soul, making us fat and sluggish with apathy toward those in need.

Look at verse 28; talk about revolting. That's an ugly picture no matter how you look at it. Now put it in the context of being practiced by God's people. That's disheartening and shameful. It shouldn't surprise us that the world operates that way, but God's people? It's nothing new to see the haves overlooking the needs of the have-nots. The haves are the ones who get, or take what they want to increase, whereas the have-nots continue to be oppressed, stepped on, stepped over, despised, and God only knows what else.

For example, day in and day out we are bombarded with commercials to buy one thing or another, and who gets the opportunity to be compensated for it? You guessed it, someone who already has the means to buy it, and not someone who needs the money. No, they need someone who has endorsement qualities, like being rich, because we have been programmed to respect those with wealth. The irony of it all is that those who can least afford it are the ones who are targeted the most for buying products that wealthy endorsers get for free. We chase after and support the endorsements of those we have come to idolize as our role models. When all we are doing is allowing ourselves to be taken advantage of by those who can care less about our situation, by influencing us to try and take part in a life that we cannot afford.

How about the many laws that are specifically designed to give those of great means the biggest tax breaks, while those who need their earned income the most receive tax relief the least. How about the wealthy who leave an inheritance for their pet but refuse to buy a meal for a beggar or homeless person. What about in the court of law? Who does the justice system work for, those with or those without? Who gets quality medical care? Whose life is valued more, and has access to better care, those with or those without? I'm not trying to give a class on sociology or human rights; I'm just trying to get us to see how true verse 28 is when it comes to man. It's just against our nature to regard and plead the cause of those in need, and that's not exclusive to wealthy people. You have poor people who despise other poor people in their condition.

Very few of us can say we have not experienced or witnessed the practice of overlooking or excusing the wickedness of the privileged because of their wealth. Nowhere do we see this practice more prominently than within our justice system. It seems that whoever can afford to pay for those who know how to find ways to balance the legal system in their favor wins. I remember reading about a crime committed, I believe in Texas, by a man who admitted to killing and dismembering another man's body. And through the manipulation of the law, his high-powered and high-paid attorneys got him acquitted of that murder. You have people of lesser means being imprisoned daily for things that would be considered misdemeanors at best in comparison to the crimes that have been committed by the wealthy.

I'm saying all these things to make one main point—some of us operate in the same manner as so many do in the world. We favor those of means within the Body of Christ, even to the point of turning a blind eye to their sins, while despising the poor among us. Consider for a moment someone you hold in high regard. Now consider someone in your church who isn't well off, who is having serious problems, doesn't dress well, has limited education, and has nothing to offer. Do you regard this person as highly as the first one you thought about? Which do you give your greatest respect? Be honest; remember God knows our heart. Many of us, including myself, would find it difficult to give a pure, unadulterated, 100 percent yes. Why can't we love and care for one another impartially? Our nature won't allow us to. We must perform it by God's nature—the Holy Spirit. Not sparingly, but often, until the power of the Holy Spirit begins to saturate our souls with God's love so our care for others will flow naturally.

Some of us need to stop using our positions and resources as tools for manipulation and control. Neither should those of us with limited resources hold those of greater means and abilities in higher regard than others, and any less accountable to God. All God's people, regardless of their station in life, are required to live obedient and holy lives (1 Peter 1:15–16).

Finally let's look at verses 30 and 31, because something is happening with God's spiritual leaders that shouldn't be. God tells Jeremiah that a "wonderful and yet horrible thing is being committed amongst His people." Not only had the people become corrupt, but God's spiritual leaders as well. The prophets no longer yielded themselves as the oracles of God, along with the priests ruling and operating by their own standards and power. What a sad and horrible sight it must have been to witness God's people sinking to such depths. Corruption and wickedness reigning throughout the camp of God's people; this is what Jeremiah was faced with continually.

God spoke to his people through Jeremiah and other

prophets, telling them of their coming judgment and to accept it (Jeremiah 21:8–10). However, some rebelled against God's judgment (Jeremiah 29:15–19) and refused to acknowledge their sins committed against God (Jeremiah 32:26–35). The nation of Israel had sunk to such depths that they had begun to practice one of the most repulsive offenses to God, idolatry. They had increased in number; they had become prosperous in the land God had promised them; they had become a strong nation, and during their highest point naturally, they fell to their lowest point spiritually and began to worship other gods. And saddest of all, the people loved having it that way. They loved following the corrupt leadership of their king and his spiritual advisers, because the spiritual leaders had become the king's men, no longer God's. They had become mouthpieces, saying what the king and people wanted to hear.

Listen to God as He speaks through Isaiah about Israel's obstinancy.

> Now go, write it before them on a table, and note it on a scroll, that it may be for the time to come forever and ever: That this is a rebellious people, lying children, children who will not hear the law of the LORD; Who say to the seers, Do not see, and to the prophets, do not prophesy to us right things; speak to us smooth things, prophesy deceits. Get you out of the way, turn aside from the path, cause the Holy

One of Israel to cease from before us.
(Isaiah 30:8–11 NKJV)

Ouch! A state that I'm certain none of us ever want to experience. I just can't imagine the torment that has to be present in the soul of a child of God who no longer desires to hear the word of God and would rather live a lie than to be in God's presence. But that's exactly what Israel had sunk to; they no longer desired the guidance of God. This attitude found its way into their hearts not during a time of poverty but at the zenith of their material prosperity. This became a great problem for God's people. Their wealth caused them to become arrogant and place their confidence more in their possessions and in themselves, than in God: "Why do you boast in the valleys, your flowing valley, O backsliding daughter? Who trusted in her treasures, saying, Who will come against me?" (Jeremiah 49:4 NKJV).

Israel had fallen victim of becoming confident in their material prosperity; a dangerous thing to do then, and just as much of a danger now, if not more so. We're beginning to see church bodies increase at an astounding rate. Rather than build more churches for different locations, you find leaders opting to build larger facilities. Undoubtedly, there are times when the growth of a church requires a larger building to accommodate their membership. The question is, as these megachurches are being built, is it being done to reach more souls or to increase the cash flow (tithes and offerings)?

As we begin to prosper financially in our ministry for God, we can be tempted to place more of our focus on marketing the word of God than proclaiming it. Profits become more of a priority than assuring that those who God intended for us to reach receive the message He has given us for their salvation and spiritual growth.

God assures us in His word that He will provide for those who labor for the furtherance of the gospel of Jesus Christ. However, His provisions are not designed for our own personal gain, but to facilitate our efforts in sharing His gospel with others. When we allow our commitment for spreading the gospel of Jesus Christ to sink to the depths of being controlled more from a profit motive than from a passion for reaching souls for Christ, we are no better than the whorish exchangers who Jesus cast out for prostituting the house of God for their own selfish gain (Matthew 21:12–13).

Distasteful as it may sound, more and more of our leaders are operating from a business venue than a ministerial one. With any structured body, business principles serve a purpose and have a place to assure a certain amount of success in managing their resources, and this reality is no different within the Body of Christ. God expects us to be faithful stewards with all our resources, especially those resources designed for the ministry. It seems now though, that quite a few of the churches within the Body of Christ have moved from a "not for profit" frame of mind to more of a corporate one.

Please don't mistake me for one who believes that God's churches, ministries, and His people are not to live anything more than a hairbreadth away from poverty. But I am suggesting that we need to be careful in not allowing ourselves to become marketing magnates, running God's church as a business—focusing more on increasing assets than increasing the lives of those God brings into the Body of Christ. Imagine the impact if God's leaders were to exert the same energy for encouraging God's people to invest in the lives of those within the Body of Christ as some of our misguided marketing wizards are exerting to increase the size of their congregation, while lining their pockets with the money they're soliciting in the name of Jesus Christ. The results would be mind-boggling.

I'm purposely using churches as an example because it appears that our teachings are beginning to gauge spiritual growth more and more with material increase, which can be very misleading. The size of a church and its wealth, as well as the personal riches of God's people, do not necessarily signify the favors of God. What's in our hearts expresses our relationship with God. When we operate by God's Spirit, it increases our heart, not diminishes it. It opens our hearts to others, not closes it. It teaches us to prefer one another and not just ourselves, or only those we like: "Be kindly affectionate to one another with brotherly love, in honor giving preference to one another" (Romans 12:10 NKJV). My brothers and sisters, our material gain is not something God wants us to concern ourselves with. Not to say that it isn't something God regards for our life, because He does care for our natural needs and wants us to increase naturally (Matthew 6:24–33). But not to the point of becoming deceived into believing that's where our values should be (Matthew 6:19–21).

As you read those verses from Matthew (chapter 6), think about how so many of us have become slaves to our possessions, holding on to them as our gods. Serving them with fear, holding onto them for dear life when, in reality, it's not ours to hold onto. We can work hard and amass as much wealth as our little minds can imagine, but let's not be duped into believing that it is what the life of Christ is based on. We may have acquired many of the things we have by living honest and productive lives, however, keep in mind that but for the grace of God, anything could have, and still can, come into our lives and snatch them in a heartbeat. I don't believe God uses wealth to confirm our life as being representative of Him. Yes, God's blessings can be expressed through wealth, but not as the main means for expressing the richness of His Spirit operating in our lives.

I don't need to tell you that being rich does not automatically make a person good, kind, and generous; life in general has taught us to know better. We need to stop this propensity of assuming that our natural prosperity is a statement for our spiritual prosperity in God. How can we, when we are turning a blind eye to the needs of those we worship with? How can we, when we are trampling over those we say we are praying for? How can we, when we do everything we can to avoid the commitment of involving ourselves in the lives of others? We can't, because we're becoming more like Israel past—fat and self-absorbed with our wealth. Following our own mind and being more confident in our own accomplishments than in God.

All is well though, because amid the greed, deceit, and confusion, God is raising up leaders who are willing to suffer the scorn of others in teaching what is right. "And I will give you shepherds according to My heart, who will feed you with knowledge and understanding" (Jeremiah 3:15 NKJV). Not shepherds who are bent on flooding us with a constant diet of prosperity teachings without the vitamins and minerals of God's Spirit. A body can be fed all the food in the world, but if the food doesn't have any nutrients for the body to absorb, it will still die. No matter how much we partake in this wave of prosperity teaching with common catch phrases: "God intends for us to be rich," "it's our destiny," "we are the head and not the tail," "name it and claim it," "it's according to your faith," "God will give us the desires of our hearts," "if you will invest in God's work he will bless you a hundredfold," "money answers all things," it all sounds good, and caught up in the right moment can be very inspiring. However, it doesn't mean a hill of beans when it comes to feeding the spiritual man. No, the way I see people latching onto this prosperity teaching seems to be more out of a love for money than a willingness to share it. And I know that isn't the operation of God's Spirit.

> But those who desire to be rich fall into temptation and a snare, and into many foolish and harmful lusts which drown men in destruction and perdition. For the love of money is a root of all kinds of evil, for which some have strayed from the faith in their greediness, and pierced themselves through with many sorrows. But thou, O man of God, flee these things and pursue righteousness, godliness, faith, love, patience, gentleness. (1 Timothy 6:9–11 NKJV)

Hear that, people of God? Hear those fruits of the Spirit (Galatians 5:22–23) being spoken to you. There's a very thin line between a desire for riches and a love for it. We should rehearse those verses from 1 Timothy 6:9–11 over and over, until they penetrate deep down into our spirit, sobering our soul to the deceptiveness of riches without the fruits of God's Spirit. God knows the pitfalls that come with wealth and the dangers of pursuing it. Many of us begin with such noble goals and intentions; however, our beginning is not what's important, but what we become in the process.

Some of us will never admit it, but the truth is that many of us can't handle real wealth, and God knows it. Think of some of the changes we've gone through out of a simple desire to become well off, believing that acquiring a certain income level will be the answer to all our concerns. In reality, oftentimes as our wealth grows, so does our desire for more possessions. We don't naturally develop a yearning to depart with our valuables. No, we usually cling to them more. What may have started off as loving of a thought as: "If God would just bless my finances, I would be able to contribute more of my time, more of my talents, more of my money," somehow ended up with us spending more time trying to preserve what we have. Rather than using it for God's glory as originally intended, we hold onto it for dear life. How can something that started off so pure become so selfish?

It's easy when a simple desire for money becomes our focus, as we're drawn across that thin line between desire and love, entangling our hearts with greed. We plunge deeper into personal gain as we gravitate further away from the spiritual things of God. Our focus on wealth becomes more burdensome than uplifting, more binding than liberating, while blinding us to our spiritual condition. We lose focus on the things we have as being God's and more as being ours, failing to entrust them back into the hands of Who they belong to in the first place.

What we need is a better understanding of how

uncertain our station in life is without God's grace for us to appreciate the blessings that come with it. As we begin to acknowledge that it is not us that establish our lives but God, then we will learn how to commit those things back to God that He has shared with us to share with others. Natural riches are fleeting at best, bearing no comparison to God's spiritual riches. If we haven't understood anything else up to this point, let us realize that as we grow closer to Christ, His richness in us should operate in such a way as to reveal His richness toward others through us. Our natural riches can never surpass God's spiritual blessings. We as God's people can fall victim to a pursuit for worldly possessions and drown in temporal pleasures or commit ourselves to those things that are more beneficial—the life of Christ and the lives of others.

3

WHEN NO ONE SEEMS TO CARE

*If a brother or sister is naked and
destitute of daily food, and one of you
says to them, "Depart in peace, be
warmed and filled," but you do not
give them the things which are needed
for the body, what does it profit?*

(JAMES 2:15–16 NKJV)

Comforting someone with words alone has little effect, if any, in resolving his or her needs. I can talk until I'm blue in the face, quote inspiring scriptures, pray the prayers of Zion, and still that will not fill empty stomachs, clothe the poor, provide shelter for the homeless, or financially assist someone who has limited resources. And yet many of us still attempt to escape our responsibility to assist others in need through pretentious words of concern.

How damaging our actions must be for those who

believe they can come to us in their hour of need, only to find out that we were more into image than deed. We project the image of compassion with words, but when someone in need comes our way, we fail in deeds. Instead of helping people recover, we set them up for hurt and disappointment. If we could just get over that propensity to hear ourselves talk, and focus more on what we do, there would be fewer wounds to heal from the disillusionment we cause.

There's urgency for God's people to come to the forefront and exhibit a genuine regard for one another. In this age of "prosperity teaching" that seemingly has flooded God's church, we are developing more of a "me-ism" attitude than a "we-ism" one. Instead of focusing on what's best for the Body of Christ, we are more concerned with our own personal interests.

Not saying that personal wealth is forbidden; however, I don't believe that God intends for it to be exclusively for our own personal benefit, "Therefore, as we have opportunity, let us do good to all, especially to those who are of the household of faith" (Galatians 6:10 NKJV). I believe that as individuals in the Body of Christ prosper, God's desire is for His church as a whole to benefit as well. Everyone within the body of Christ will not be wealthy. However, I do believe that if we were to entrust our resources to God for His purpose, we as a people can reap from the blessings of others.

Will this ever become a reality in this life within Christ's church? I cannot say for certain; only God knows. Do I believe God's people can function as a body having a common interest in each other's welfare? Yes. Why it's not happening now can be attributed to many reasons. But I dare not attempt to list them all. Only God has the knowledge and ability to do that. However, I would like to share with you what I believe God has given me to help those who may be feeling a sense of hopelessness in the possibility of anyone ever caring.

It May Be God's Plan

What I'm about to discuss may not be of much comfort initially, but if you hear me out, it could be of significant use during our valleys of despair. Not many things can be as hopeless as to have a need, and no one seems to care.

Before I go any further, let me point out that throughout this book I will be using the terms "need," or "needs," and when I do, it isn't predicated on just the financial, but whatever things that may be needed for a person's well-being.

Believe it, saints of God, our Father sometimes plans desert places for us for His own personal glory. And no matter how strong our desire is for someone's help, it's all for naught until God's purpose has been fulfilled. Joseph suffered many hardships to accomplish God's purpose in preserving Israel during the ensuing drought. Job suffered great losses—family, possessions, friends, and even a sense of God's presence—to accomplish God's purpose in proving his reverence to Him. Jonah was not spared from his trials in preparation for God's purpose in saving the nation of Nineveh from certain destruction. And all these instances had one thing in common—they glorified God.

Let's probe deeper into Job's situation in hopes that we will get a better understanding of what I'm trying to say. When the tragedies began to come into Job's life, he was living an upright and perfect life before God (Job 1:1). Now don't misconstrue the word *perfect* as to suggest Job lived a perfect life absent of faults and mistakes. No Job missed the mark sometimes in his attempt to live righteously before God like all of us still do today. What is being said is that Job governed his life in such a way as to honor and revere God. He lived a spiritually mature life before God. And, yes, spiritually mature people have faults like anyone else. The only person I can attest to that lived a faultless life before God was Jesus. And we're not expected to be Christ, but we are to submit to God's will like Christ: "Let this mind be in you, which was also in Christ Jesus" (Philippians 2:5 NKJV).

I'm certain that as Job's situation intensified, so did his hope for some form of relief. It would only be natural for Job to look to those whom he felt close to for comfort. But if you've read the book of Job, you know that was not the case.

Not to say that those closest to Job were deliberately callous and insensitive to his needs, although at times it appears that way, but as we learn from reading Job, God had a purpose for Job's suffering (Job 1:6–12, 2:1–6). I would like for you to read those scriptures at least one more time before reading what I have to say about Job 2:3 NKJV.

> Then the Lord said to Satan, Have you considered My servant Job, that there is none like him on the earth, a blameless and upright man, one who fears God and shuns evil? And still he holds fast to his integrity, although you incited Me against him, to destroy him without cause.

This is the second time mentioned of God bringing Satan's attention to Job (Job 1:8). Why? God had purposely designed this occasion for His glory by proving Job's reverence to Him. And how did Job show his reverence to God? By devoting himself to living a righteous life before God.

It can be difficult accepting the consequences of our faults, no matter how much we realize it was of our own doing. Now try to imagine dealing with hardships that you have no control of, nor understand. God knew His purpose for Job's sufferings, but Job didn't. God knew that Satan desired to destroy Job, even before God presented Satan with the opportunity to express it. And just as in the days of Job, Satan desires to destroy all who belong to God and dare to live for Him. If Satan had his way, he would like to destroy everyone. But he has a more intense hatred for those who belong to God that live devoted lives for Him.

There are going to be times when God has designed situations in our lives that are expressly for His glory. Not to destroy us, but to prove us, and glorify God.

There's not a trial I can recall that, after God brought me through it, I didn't benefit from it. Whether it was of my own doing, poor judgment, disobedience, or specifically designed by God, God out of His infinite grace and mercy would use it for my good and His glory (Romans 8:28).

Throughout God's word, you read where God turned the situations of His people for His glory and their good. In the Old Testament, whenever God passed judgment upon Israel, God did not set them up for destruction, even though many of them lost their lives from His judgment, but God set them up for repentance, so that He could redeem them as His people. God does the same today. Rather than destroying us in our disobedience, He redeems us for His glory. Now if God redeems us even in our disobedience, how much more then in His purposely designed situations for us.

The key is that we learn to trust God in whatever situation we find ourselves in, knowing that He is controlling whatever is allowed to come into our lives: "Trust in the Lord with all your heart, and lean not on your own understanding. In all your ways acknowledge Him, and he shall direct your paths" (Proverbs 3:5–6 NKJV). This trust in God was essential for Job to endure

Tariek Gahiji

the hardships he suffered for God's glory. Read the sentiments of Job in chapter 19. Talk about depressing emotions. However, look at how Job expresses his continued confidence in God: "For I know that my Redeemer lives, and He shall stand at last on the earth; And after my skin is destroyed, this I know, that in my flesh I shall see God, Whom I shall see for myself, and my eyes shall behold, and not another. How my heart yearns within me" (Job 19:25–27 NKJV). What faith and dedication Job expresses for God.

Job has lost everything—his children, support of his friends and wife, respect in the community—and through it all, Job never loses his trust in God. He looks to God as his Redeemer and places his confidence in God to preserve his life, even though his body may be consumed and destroyed.

Can we honestly say that we would do the same? All our children tragically gone, friendless, disdainful mate, persecuted and disrespected by everyone we meet, and to all this, illnesses with seemingly no remedies or cures in sight. Could we? Would we? If we sincerely consider the severity of Job's situation, we would be very careful in saying yes, to say the least, and more than likely would rather not have to answer this question at all.

And yet some of us have and will face hardships that seem to be beyond human endurance. And the question remains, how do we handle hardships that outwardly have no sense of purpose or explanation? Trust in God with all our heart, and take no confidence in our feeble attempts to comprehend or define those things we don't understand. But in everything acknowledge God as our Redeemer as Job did, and I have no doubts that God will provide us with the same grace he provided for Job.

It's not about our weakness in trying times but about our attitude. Job grew weak at times, but he never lost his confidence in God. If he had, he would have turned away from God, rather than going before him in prayer. Even in his complaints, Job was exhibiting his trust in God. For I don't believe that Job was charging anything against God but was looking to God for some sort of relief for the many hardships he was experiencing.

We're not always going to be able to rejoice, praise, and give thanks in our trials, and don't think for one moment God doesn't realize and understand this. That's just our human side wearing down, which is why we must look to God for his grace as Job did. To help us hold on as He uses our adversities to perfect in us the spiritual maturity needed for enduring greater challenges: "But may the God of all grace, Who called us to His eternal glory by Christ Jesus, after that ye have suffered a while, perfect, establish, strengthen, and settle you" (1 Peter 5:10 NKJV).

Paul also grew weary of situations in his life. One in particular is worth mentioning, because I believe it highlights our vulnerability to the weaknesses that lies within us without God's grace. In (2 Corinthians

12:7–10), Paul speaks on how God allowed an affliction in his flesh to exist, not to destroy him, but to keep him from falling prey to self-exaltation through the flesh, due to the many revelations that God had shared with him.

Paul expresses his displeasure for this affliction by his continued petitions before God to remove it, until God answers him not with a relief of the affliction but with a means by which to endure it. What is being conveyed to Paul, as well as to God's people, is that spiritual maturity is developed through acknowledgement of our weaknesses and frailties to God, and not by superficial acts of strength.

So rather than grieve over his infirmities, Paul says that he will glory in them. Not to the extent of looking for ways to exhibit weaknesses, but to seek and receive the power of God. What am I trying to say here? I'm trying to express the reality that we are going to grow weary and tired sometimes of situations in our lives. And that's expected of flesh. But what we are not to do is grow so weak that we stop seeking God for His grace. We are to petition our Father as often as needed, with expectancy and hope, knowing that He is our Savior and will deliver us from every situation that comes into our lives according to His agenda, while preserving us as He fulfills His purpose.

It May Be You

As distasteful as it may be, there are times when people's insensitivity may stem from our conduct. Let's be truthful, for some of us we're not the most likable person in the basket. We're like that rotten apple that if not removed will affect the other apples. So, people tend to avoid us not because they don't love us; they just don't like us.

Does that sound like genuine love? How can you love someone and not like them? Well, it's not that you're not liked as a person; it's your ways that are hard to deal with. Some of us have offensive natures that drive people away from us. And sadly, when someone loves us enough to let us know of our offensive ways, we often take offense to it. Isn't that odd that the offender would take offense to being told they are being offensive. Whatever our character flaws are, it's unlikely that people are going to like them.

Since man's creation, throughout the Bible we read of instances where God expresses His displeasure with our behavior. We also read of times when God withdrew His favor from His people due to continued disobedience. Understanding this about God is crucial to accepting that no one is expected to like offenses. As God's people, we may have to tolerate them, but excusing them is unlikely.

Let me clarify the difference between tolerating and excusing offenses. When you tolerate a thing, you endure what's necessary to deal with it until it can be corrected or removed. Now for someone to endure our distasteful ways usually takes one of the fruits of the Spirit called long-suffering. We need to understand this to avoid the "pity parties" we like to have when no one seems to care. In other words, no one is always going to be long-suffering toward our offensive nature.

It's amazing that however unlikable we may be, we still expect people to rally around us in our time of need. And to a certain degree, we're right. Within the Body of Christ, we should be able to receive the love needed to help us through life's trials regardless of our personality. After all, God still loves us in our worst state: "But God demonstrates His own love toward us, in that while we were still sinners, Christ died for us" (Romans 5:8 NKJV). If you should be so blessed as to have someone who can look beyond your faults and respond to your needs, be appreciative of God's love operating in them.

Now we should never expect anyone to excuse our offenses or treat our offensive behavior as though it never happened. It's not humanly possible to wound someone without them feeling some sort of pain. Neither can you offend someone without him or her experiencing some degree of hurt. So, when people respond to us in different ways when we're hurting, consider the source of their behavior. Are their actions being influenced by some prior acts of ours? Don't be so farsighted when it comes to other people's actions, and so shortsighted when it comes to yours:

And why do you look at the speck in your brother's eye, but do not consider the plank in your own eye? Or how can you say to your brother, "Let me remove the speck from your eye"; and look, a plank is in your own eye? Hypocrite! First remove the plank from your own eye, and then you will see clearly to remove the speck from your brother's eye. (Matthew 7:3–5 NKJV)

It's so easy to crucify people for their actions when it comes to how they treat us and yet so difficult to clearly see how we treat them.

Computer technicians have a saying: "Garbage in, garbage out," which means the quality of information you put into a computer is the quality of information you get out of it. Now, God's word clearly admonishes us against returning "evil for evil" (Romans 12:17). And God's word also warns us that "we reap what we sow" (Galatians 6:7). So, those who are offended as well as those who offend should keep these two passages of scripture in mind when dealing with one another. If you recompense evil for evil, you will reap what you sow. And those who carelessly offend will bear the fruit of their offenses, for what you put out will be your reward.

When I was a child, I used to hear my mother say, "You draw more bees with honey." It took me some years to fully understand what she meant. But now I understand that if you want people to be more loving toward you, you must also be lovable. Why would you expect to receive roses when all you give are thorns? Life just doesn't flow that way. If you give flowers for people's lives, you'll at least be able to enjoy the fragrance of them.

It's not always easy addressing our faults. But address them we must if we want to reap the harvest of God's favor. You can't continue to excuse or cover your offenses and expect to prosper in God: "He who covers his sins will not prosper, but whoever confesses and forsakes them will have mercy" (Proverbs 28:13 NKJV).

Stop protecting your hostile nature and deal with it. Don't allow flesh weaknesses to continue pampering what God's Spirit desires to cleanse: "If we confess our sins, He is faithful and just to forgive us our sins and to cleanse us from all unrighteousness" (1 John 1:9 NKJV).

Not meaning to cleanse us from all possible sin because that's an ongoing process until we leave our mortal bodies. But upon true repentance of an offense, God will thoroughly cleanse us of our desire to continue in the offense we confess.

To look at "all unrighteousness" as meaning to remove all tendencies to sin is incorrect and irrational. For if we examine ourselves, we'll know that's not possible. But what is possible is to acknowledge our sins when brought to our awareness and not avoid them.

One very common practice I've experienced among

God's people is the tendency to excuse our offenses through forgiveness. We'll say that God forgives us and so should others when we're faced with addressing a fault of our own. It's true that as Christ's examples, those within the Body of Christ must forgive one another for offenses: "For if you forgive men their trespasses, your heavenly Father will also forgive you. But if you do not forgive men their trespasses, neither will your Father forgive your trespasses" (Matthew 6:14–15 NKJV).

This is not an option but a command. However, this truth does not excuse us of the accountability for our actions. We're still responsible for what we do no matter how much we are required to forgive one another. There are many scriptures we can refer to for receiving forgiveness of our offenses; however, know this, there are just as many scriptures if not more that instruct us of our responsibility to deal with the offenses we commit.

There's one more issue I'd like to discuss. And that is the practice of trying to use God's word to manipulate our way around addressing or correcting our offensive behavior. Whenever we deceive ourselves into believing that we can use God's word to make a plea for a fault or weakness, we run the risk of developing insensitivity to God's Spirit. Stop resisting the truth of God's word to avoid falling victim to your own lies.

Sadly, there are people who try so hard to defend their offenses rather than correct them that they start lying to avoid confessing them. This is a terrible state to fall into. Whether lying to others or to ourselves, we should never take it lightly. And there's no such thing as a little lie. Lies don't come in degrees—a lie is a lie. God hates lying and takes great offense to its practice (Proverbs 6:16–19, 12:22).

Lying has a nature of its own, and the only resolution for it is the truth. God's strong hatred for it should serve as a deterrent against resorting to any form of lying. There is never a good time to lie because one lie leads to another. Have you ever told a lie and not had to tell another lie to support the one told? The natural flow of lying is to tell more lies to conceal the ones you tell. And the result is eventually getting entangled by our own web of lies (Proverbs 5:22).

We need to take a sincere inventory of ourselves before making the necessary changes for becoming more pleasing in the sight of God and humans. Objectionable behavior isn't something that people tend to embrace. And people seldom gain the favor of those that reject them. Some of us know that we have ways that are offensive, and rather than address them, we choose to charge people with being insensitive to our needs. Try to be more pleasing in the sight of others to enhance every opportunity of receiving someone's compassion in your time of need.

To Those Who Don't

Some of us don't have a genuine concern for other people's welfare. I've been blessed to serve in churches where on a good day you might have twenty-five people for Sunday service; at another church hundreds; and even thousands at another church. And one thing I have learned is that it's not the size of the church that determines how much we care, but the content of our hearts. From one of the smallest of churches to one of the largest, I've witnessed, too often, a lack of genuine concern for people's needs.

Why would I make such a statement? Well, in my journey with Christ, I've seen people exert great energy in ignoring the needs of others. We've all been guilty of doing it one time or another, but my concern is for those of us who have made a practice of it.

What's most sobering of all is it doesn't matter whether we're rich or poor that determines our willingness to show compassion. I've seen poor people exhibit less concern for those who are in the same condition they're in. You would think their related situation would produce a more positive response toward one another. I've also observed the unwillingness of those who were well off to share their resources with those in desperate need. And I'm not just talking about people outside the Body of Christ, but those who claim to be a member of the Body of Christ.

I believe the main purpose for God inspiring me to

write this book is to express the need for His people to become more of an example of addressing the needs of people as Christ intended:

> Then the King will say to those on His right hand, Come, you blessed of My Father, inherit the kingdom prepared for you from the foundation of the world: For I was hungry and you gave Me food; I was thirsty and you gave Me drink; I was a stranger and you took Me in; I was naked and you clothed Me; I was sick and you visited Me; I was in prison and you came to Me. Then the righteous will answer Him, saying, Lord, when did we see You hungry and feed You, or thirsty and give You drink? When did we see You a stranger and take You in, or naked and clothe You? Or when did we see You sick, or in prison, and come to You? And the King will answer and say to them, Assuredly, I say to you, inasmuch as you did it to one of the least of these My brethren, you did it to Me. (Matthew 25:34–40 NKJV)

The whole of this parable is (Matthew 25:31–46). I specifically used this portion of the parable to reveal how sensitive of a matter it is to Jesus Christ that we put forth an effort to care for others. So much so that Jesus looks upon our regard for others as a vested interest in Him. That's an awesome thought to keep in mind as we go about living our lives for Christ.

Also take note of how Jesus refers to them as His brethren. I think of a twofold purpose for Jesus doing so. First, we should take special interest in caring for those who are in the Body of Christ. And secondly, in the real world we should know that everyone we meet having a need will not always belong to Christ; however, we still are required to address their needs whenever possible (Galatians 6:10). The question is, are we truly caring for one another as Christ desires us to? And do we really have the heart of Jesus working within us? If we say yes, then Jesus's compassion for others should spring forth from our lives as living waters.

Let's look at verse 37 of the parable in (Matthew 25:31–46). Notice how Jesus addresses those who exhibit the character of caring for those in need as the righteous. Does this mean that Jesus is saying they are righteous of themselves? No. God's word clearly points out that our righteousness is as filthy rags to him. When Jesus refers to them as being righteous, I believe He is directing our attention more toward the acts in Matthew 25:35–36 that they carried out for those in need. I believe Jesus is letting us know that those who live righteous lives will freely help those in need.

For certain Jesus is also talking about those who have been justified through His blood sacrifice on the cross. The distinction is clearly stated at the end of the parable in Matthew 25:46, as to those who belong to Christ and those who don't. But I don't believe this parable was specifically purposed for letting us know how we receive salvation but was designed more so to reveal to us the character one exhibits that identifies with or lives for Christ.

As the Body of Christ, what we do here on earth has a lot to do with our eternal rewards. I'd like to look at a scripture that is often used for instructing us against using our bodies as instruments of sin:

> Now if anyone builds on this foundation with gold, silver, precious stones, wood, hay, straw, each one's work will become clear; for the Day will declare it, because it will be revealed by fire; and the fire will test each one's work, of what sort it is. If anyone's work which he has built on it endures, he shall receive a reward. If anyone's work is burned, he will suffer loss: but he himself will be saved, yet so as through fire. (1 Corinthians 3:12–15 NKJV)

The foundation spoken of in verse 12 is Jesus Christ, and when you read chapter 3 of 1 Corinthians, you will better understand that what is being addressed is our responsibility for producing spiritual works with God's temple, which is our body. And that is the point I am fervently trying to convey—the significance of performing spiritual works in our lives. When we direct our attentions and efforts toward alleviating the needs of others, we are performing spiritual works that build upon the spiritual foundation of Christ—works that will not be destroyed but will endure into eternity.

Having the righteousness of Christ (His Spirit) dwelling within us doesn't automatically bring forth righteous acts. We must intentionally respond to God's Spirit to bring the desired results. Two situations come to mind when I think of our struggle with caring for others. One is when we know in our mind it is the right thing to do, and yet it's not in our heart to do so, and the other is when it's in our heart to care, and our mind resists the desires of our heart.

I believe what's in a man's heart is more important than what is in his mind. From my own experience, I've found myself more prone to act upon the things that penetrate my heart, than the things that enter my mind. There have been many things that I have thought about and nothing resulted from it. But those things that would permeate my heart would also come with a passion to fulfill it. For I believe that God's Spirit speaks to our heart to govern our mind: "Keep your heart with all diligence; for out of it spring the issues of life" (Proverbs 4:23 NKJV).

I'm not suggesting that our thoughts are of little consequence to what we do. What I am saying is that when they become attached to our heart is when they are likely to be carried out. Jesus points this out in a scripture regarding adultery: "You have heard that it was said to those of old: You shall not commit adultery.

But I say to you that whoever looks at a woman to lust for her has already committed adultery with her in his heart" (Matthew 5:27–28 NKJV). Notice how Jesus mentions the heart and not the mind. Understand that lusts are uncontrolled desires that have reached our hearts. And I believe the significance of what Jesus is telling us is that once it gets into our heart, it is as good as done. With this in mind, why not allow thoughts of kindness to penetrate our hearts and not just remain on the surface of our minds. You don't have to have Christ's righteousness dwelling in you to perform random acts of kindness, people are doing that daily. But to passionately perform selfless acts of caring for someone else's welfare is what God desires from His ambassadors of hope.

In this time, it is more than a notion taking on the challenge of regarding other people's needs as a major concern in our lives. However, this is what God requires of His people: "Let love be without hypocrisy. Abhor what is evil. Cling to what is good. Be kindly affectionate to one another with brotherly love, in honor giving preference to one another ... distributing to the needs of the saints, given to hospitality" (Romans 12:9–10, 13 NKJV). If we apply these scriptures to our lives as they are expressed, we shouldn't have any problems in serving the needs of others. But for clarification purposes, let's probe a little deeper in hopes of getting a better understanding of what Paul is saying to us. To "let love be without hypocrisy" is to say that our love is to be without pretense. In other words, our love should be sincere. Do I really need to explain our hating evil and adhering to what is good?

Verse 10 is what I desire for us to take a closer look at before going to Romans 12:13. The words "kindly affectionate" both suggest a kindred or more intimate type of relationship toward one another. And when you add "brotherly love" to it, it's rather difficult not seeing how we are to have a deeper concern for each other's welfare. Just in case we do, let's try dissecting the second part of verse 10 and see what we come up with. "In honor giving preference to one another"—the honor that is being spoken of here is one of high regard for another. To do that usually requires humility from the one showing the honor. And the word "preference" from *The New Strong's Exhaustive Concordance of the Bible"* gives the Greek definition—to lead the way for others (i.e., show deference). *Merriam Webster's Collegiate Dictionary/Tenth Edition*, defines the word *deference* as respect and esteem due a superior or an elder.

Okay, let's try to make sense of all these definitions and see if we can come up with a clearer understanding of Romans 12:10. First, the honor and preference we are to show is toward one another and not just to those who we may regard as holding a higher station in life, office, or title. Am I saying that we are not to honor and respect certain positions that God has ordained others with such as pastors, elders, evangelists, and the like?

I proclaim an emphatic no! However, I am saying that we are not to regard one's welfare, or person, as more important than another's. We are all precious in the sight of God, and He doesn't consider one person's welfare more important than another's. God forbids us to show partiality, regardless of one's state (Leviticus 19:15).

As we apply these definitions to Romans 12:10, we can safely say that we are to exhibit kindred (intimate) spirits of brotherly love toward everyone. With high regard for each other's welfare, we should strive to satisfy the needs of others and not just our own. Which leads into the final verse of interest (Romans 12:13), and that is that we are to address the needs of God's people as God's people. We should welcome and receive them into our lives, instead of turning them away.

Are we always going to be able to meet the needs of others? Probably not, but too many of us are turning a deaf ear to the cries of those in dire need, and that just shouldn't be. We know their needs, and yet we do everything we can to justify why we didn't address them. We can keep on fooling ourselves, but we can't fool God because He knows our hearts.

There's no harm, or danger, in preferring someone else's best interest above our own. I know that is a hard statement for many of us to conceive. Honestly, from a logical standpoint, it is downright foolish. However, we need to understand that we're not dealing with logic but with the ways of God. Logically, I'd be silly to place someone else's needs above my own, and yet there may be times when God will ask this of me. The question is will I trust God enough to do it? The widow did with Elijah (1 Kings 17:8–16), but most importantly, Jesus Christ did for our salvation. So much so that He placed our welfare above His very life.

Just as God spoke to the heart of the widow to address the needs of Elijah first and to trust in Him in making provisions for her out of her obedience to His will. God also requires that same trust and obedience from us, when He places other people's needs in our paths. And please don't play off that familiar line we tend to use: "How will I know it's the Lord?" If you are willing to yield to the anointing of God's Spirit as the widow did, you'll know.

Am I saying that we are to go about our lives sacrificing our welfare for everyone else's? No. We have responsibilities to ourselves, and some of us to our children and spouses. What I am saying is that too often we neglect the people that God often places before us, by dodging their needs. If we were playing dodge ball, some of us would never get hit, because we have become so skillful in avoiding the avenues that would lead to our responding to other people's needs. Lord hit us on the head with one of your balls of understanding, please Lord, and do it now.

Every one of us can probably think of a time when we should have addressed someone else's needs. The reality is we just weren't willing to sacrifice our desires for their needs. And that is so sad. Earlier I mentioned how God would sometime place us in positions of preferring the needs of others before our own. I not only firmly believe that, but I also believe it is God's will to do so. But there are times when we won't do for others even when we are able, purely out of an act of selfishness. Rather than defer some of the things we want, we'll label them as needs to dance around our responsibility to help. Oh, so sad, so sad.

If we could only come to the realization of how blessed we are when given the opportunity to be a blessing for others. God doesn't desire for us to only pray for ourselves but for other people as well. And those who have learned the value of prayer have also learned how much more of a blessing it is to pray for others than just for themselves. It's somewhat mind-boggling how many of our prayers tend to get answered before we petition God for them, when we pray for someone else. Just as our prayer life should be considerate of other people's lives, so should our acts of kindness and charity.

To better understand the blessings of giving, you must first learn to give freely. I think of a scripture I hear quoted so often by others: "Give, and it will be given to you: good measure, pressed down, shaken together, and running over will be put into your bosom. For with the same measure that you use, it will be measured back to you" (Luke 6:38 NKJV). This is a very reassuring promise from God if we apply it properly and sincerely. Sadly, many of us attempt to use this scripture to get something in return for our giving. And I don't believe that's the message Jesus is conveying to us.

I believe Jesus is letting us know how rewarding it can be when we give freely, expecting nothing in return. Not using our giving as a bargaining tool to receive from God or from anyone else but purely out of a desire to please God by doing His will: "But love your enemies, do good, and lend, hoping for nothing in return; and your reward will be great, and you will be sons of the Most High. For He is kind to the unthankful and evil. Therefore be merciful, just as your Father also is merciful" (Luke 6:35–36 NKJV). That's heavy, people of God. Not only does God desire for us to give to our enemy, but in doing so, to give it freely expecting nothing in return. For many of us, it's difficult to lend to those who are close to us, and we expect to get what we loan them back. But Jesus tells us to do this for our enemies. Now if God expects us to be this merciful and kind toward our enemies expecting nothing in return, how much more so for our brothers and sisters in Christ. I guess the question is are we willing to make the sacrifices necessary to exercise the mercy our Father gives to us? Read Luke 6:27–38 in hopes of getting a better idea of how Jesus instructs us to govern ourselves. As difficult as it may be to exercise what is said in those scriptures, I believe God means exactly what is written. So it is written, so it shall be done. Amen.

We can receive so much more from God if we will just free our hearts of selfish giving to godly giving. It grieves my heart greatly when I see people trying to bargain for God's blessings. It can't be done because God's blessings are free. There are leaders today, some unknowingly and some intentionally, influencing people to give monetary offerings in hopes of being healed or receiving financial blessings in return for their donations. How often have we seen prayer lines being formed based on the promises of healings and financial blessings through monetary contributions to someone else's ministry? Or how about this one: "Send in a love offering" and they will send you a blessed cloth, hanky, or container of water assuring your healing or some monetary gain. The truth of the matter is that nothing could be further from the truth. And those who are using these tactics to swindle the unsuspecting souls who are desperately seeking resolutions to their problems will answer to God for resorting to such practices. When you find someone focused more on how much you give from a monetary standpoint than from a commitment to giving your life to Christ, be wary.

What I'm trying to get us to understand is that giving freely with a pure heart is very important to God. If we are giving with the wrong motives, our giving is in vain concerning receiving the promises of God about our giving. When we give without God's purpose (will) in mind, we more than likely will not be in line to receive

His blessings. Why? Well, our express purpose of giving should be to glorify God. And when we glorify God, we please Him. Do we need a scholarly dissertation as to what happens when we are pleasing (loving) to our Father? Every one of us who has been blessed to have a relationship with our parents have learned that they gave more freely to us when our ways were pleasing to them. How much more does this truth apply to God our Father:

> And whatever we ask we receive from Him, because we keep His commandments and do those things that are pleasing in His sight. And this is His commandment: that we should believe on the name of His Son Jesus Christ and love one another, as He gave us commandment. Now he who keeps His commandments abides in Him, and He in him. And by this we know that He abides in us, by the Spirit whom He has given us. (1 John 3:22–24 NKJV)

Are we doing those things that God asks of us to please Him? If we believe in Jesus Christ as God commands us to, then we must believe in the things He instructs us to do. If we love one another as God commands us to, then we should have no problem with addressing one another's needs. If God's Spirit dwells (actively lives) in us, then we shouldn't have a problem with submitting to God's will. And if people are not seeing the Spirit of God actively moving in our lives, the only conclusion I can come to is that we are resisting God's Spirit: "Do not quench the Spirit" (1 Thessalonians 5:19 NKJV). The word *quench*, according to *The New Strong's Exhaustive Concordance of The Bible*, means to extinguish, and sad to say, so many of us have resisted God's Spirit for so long that we no longer respond to His urgings.

4

WE ARE FAMILY

And Adam called his wife's name Eve,
because she was the mother of all living.

(GENESIS 3:20 NKJV)

I remember while growing up how my parents would let relatives live with us. Many of them had migrated from the South looking for a better life in Chicago. No matter how often they had to take someone in, it never seemed to be an issue of letting them live at our home.

This practice wasn't something only my parents did. It was quite common among many families within the community where I lived. When loved ones were trying to make a better life for themselves, or just simply needed some place to stay, family members had no problem placing out the welcome mat.

And now as I look back from a more mature perspective, I realize that along with my parents, many of those who shared their homes were not all that well off. But they had a strong sense of family. So much so that other family members who didn't have to share their homes would contribute whatever they could to help those that did.

I remember my parents sharing with me and my brother how when they moved from the South, another family shared their home with us until my father could afford and find a place of our own. We were babies then—my brother two years old and me only two weeks old. And the beauty of it all was that they were not blood relatives but were kind enough to open their hearts and home to us.

With each passing generation, we seemingly move that much further from that common thread we once shared as family members called kinship. That virtual bond that wouldn't have allowed us to be comfortable with the pseudo relationships we have grown accustomed to. This widespread disconnect of family weakens the once stable nuclear family and endangers whatever remnant of the extended family we have left.

Unfortunately, this truth challenges God's family as well. This failure to bond with one another as family has often caused divisions rather than the unity Jesus Christ prayed for. I'm not saying that the Body of Christ is in total disarray. No way. My God is much bigger than that. But that doesn't negate the fact that there are divisions between family members within the Body of Christ. Rather than becoming the nuclear and extended family God created us to be, some of us are drifting further apart. Are we living as the close-knit family God intended? And if not, how do we get there? Prayerfully with God's guidance, we'll develop a better understanding of what He expects of us as a family in this chapter.

Different Tribe/Same Family

According to the Bible, God created man, and out of man He created woman. And through that union God created humans. As I ponder man's origin, and for those of us who believe in the Holy Bible as being the inspired word of God, it amazes me how divided we are as a people. According to God's word we all are descendants of the seed of Adam and sprung from the womb of Eve: "And Adam called his wife's name Eve, because she was the mother of all living" (Genesis 3:20 NKJV). Therefore, Adam and Eve is God's origin for natural birth as we know it. So why do we have such a difficult time with identifying with one another?

From an outward perspective, there is no doubt that differences are apparent. From skin color to culture, nationality, customs, language, and beliefs, the list of differences can become extensive if we choose to take that route. But how much are we aware of the one common factor that truly matters? And that is that we're all God's creation through Adam and Eve. And regardless of the many different features between us, we all have one thing in common. We're all human beings comprising humanity. We all have the same basic biological makeup and needs that distinguish humans from any other creation.

Since humans' spiritual separation from God, Satan has been promoting division between us throughout every generation. He's used every venue available to him. Some of the most common yet denied ones are nationality, creed, culture, and skin color. After close examination of the endless conflicts that have transpired between humankind, you'll find that most if not all have been influenced by one of these factors.

Being the most intelligent of God's creation on earth, it's amazing how we incessantly find things to be at odds with. The lower creations on earth who God had intended for us to rule over seem to have a better view of cohabitation than we do. For most of them only come into conflict with one another out of a necessity for survival. Whereas with man we seem to have an insatiable desire to purposely find differences between ourselves rather than focus on the things we have in common.

Man has been at odds with God and each other since that initial disobedient act of Adam resulting in our spiritual separation from God. And that division and separation will remain for those who haven't received Jesus Christ as their Savior. But most disturbing are the divisions that are so prevalent within the Body of Christ that shouldn't be.

As God's people, some of the same national pride,

customs, beliefs, and practices that once influenced us while in the world continue to do so within the Body of Christ. Tribal warfare is nothing new per se because throughout history we can read about nations battling with each other for supremacy. But as God's people, we are supposed to be a beacon of peace and unity for the world.

We're all individuals with distinct personalities that make up multiple nationalities, which practice different customs and beliefs. However, God views all of us as His creation. And as born-again Christians, we're viewed as individuals on a higher plane as God's spiritual family—still having distinct personalities but possessing God's Spirit, making us one with God and each other:

> For as the body is one and has many members, but all the members of that one body, being many, are one body, so also is Christ. For by one Spirit we were all baptized into one body, whether Jews or Greeks, whether slaves or free; and have all been made to drink into one Spirit. For in fact the body is not one member but many. (1 Corinthians. 12:12–14 NKJV)

With all our uniqueness and diversity, we're intimately connected by God's Spirit through our rebirth. We're more than a natural family; we've been moved to a much higher plane as a spiritual family. Our family ties are much deeper now for they are eternal.

These ties within the Body of Christ are so relevant that they supersede all natural ties. Listen to Jesus when He proclaims who His family is:

> While He was still talking to the multitudes, behold, His mother and brothers stood outside, seeking to speak with Him. Then one said to Him, "Look, Your mother and Your brothers are standing outside, seeking to speak with You." But He answered and said to the one who told Him, "Who is My mother and who are My brothers?" And He stretched out His hand toward His disciples and said, "Here are My mother and My brothers! For whoever does the will of My Father in heaven is My brother and sister and mother." (Matthew 12:46–50 NKJV)

Jesus makes it very clear that to be considered part of His family, you must be obedient to God's will. And God's will is for every one of us to be spiritually born again through the gift of our Lord and Savior Jesus Christ.

Now God is not asking those of us who have been spiritually translated into the Body of Christ to sever our ties with our natural family. But we need to understand that our spiritual family ties hold more value than our natural family. And unless those within our natural family receive Jesus Christ as their Savior as well, there will be an eternal separation after our death.

The main thing is that we need to understand that our oneness in Christ supersedes our differences. By God's Spirit we are to move beyond our differences functioning as His spiritual family expressing unity rather than divisions.

The Great Divide

Today you have more churches identifying themselves as nondenominational, multiracial, and multiethnic. This is good for the Body of Christ. But with that identity, does it express distinction or unity?

I've been to nondenominational, multiracial, and multiethnic churches, and there's one thing I've seen more commonly practiced than not, and that is people tend to group with their nationality. So, I ask the question: What is being taught about the unity of God's family?

Paul addressed this matter in his letters to the Galatian and Colossian church:

> For you are all sons of God through faith in Christ Jesus. For as many of you as were baptized into Christ have put on Christ. There is neither Jew nor Greek, there is neither slave nor free, there is neither male

nor female; for you are all one in Christ Jesus." (Galatians 3:26–28 NKJV)

Where there is neither Greek nor Jew, circumcised nor uncircumcised, barbarian, Scythian, slave nor free, but Christ is all and in all. (Colossians 3:11 NKJV)

Paul clearly dismisses all practices of making distinctions within the Body of Christ. A church's identity should not be expressed by cultural makeup but by its spiritual relationship with Jesus Christ and each other. Being multiethnic, multicultural, nondenomination, or whatever other title used to express an indiscriminate position is wonderful. But proclaiming to be a Christian church says it all.

This has great significance regarding our relationship to one another. Scripture says that whoever God's Holy Spirit does not dwell in is not His (Romans 8:9). Those within the Body of Christ not only have relationship with Christ but with each other. Nationality, ethnicity, and gender don't matter; what matters is the bond we have through Jesus Christ (1 Corinthians 12:12–13).

I remember a minister years ago saying that there was nothing wrong with preferring your own nationality. It was only natural to do so. I agreed with him then because of my limited understanding at the time of God's view of us as His. The only thing I agree with now is that it is natural. However, it has no place spiritually within God's family. And our practicing it is unacceptable before God.

Within the Body of Christ there are no distinctions, just likeness. Our likeness in Jesus Christ and kinship with each other is what we should be rejoicing in. Ancestral, cultural, native, and gender differences make up one of Satan's most instrumental tools used against humankind to cause divisions.

It's not something we like discussing, but with the rise of more multicultural churches we need to. Whether we want to admit it or not, some of us consciously as well as unconsciously respond to our innate prejudices every day. It just seems to have more of a bitter taste when we associate it with God's church. However, prejudice is not as ugly as some of us make it, because in general it's nothing more than showing preference. But since God does not have respect of persons, neither should we.

What God desires for us is to view one another as Christians because in doing so that designates us as belonging to Jesus Christ. It doesn't designate any religion, denomination, culture, nationality, or gender—just Jesus Christ and those who are believers and followers of Him. You will have those who will try to do otherwise, but God's word does not affiliate Christianity with anyone but Jesus Christ and His church.

This is not as simple as it sounds because before our salvation, we had years of seeing things according to the world. And now we must learn to see things according to God and His word. This doesn't happen overnight and without a conscious effort and commitment to do so with the power of God's Spirit. God is not going to make us view each other as brothers and sisters in Christ, but with our salvation and His Holy Spirit, we can.

There was a time when acknowledging my African descent was important to me. But as God began to open my understanding as to who I really am since my salvation, what matters now is that I am a Christian (Holy Spirit filled believer and follower of Jesus Christ). And that's how I plan to practice seeing all those who belong to Jesus Christ until it becomes a mind-set and no longer a determination.

One of the main things Israel fell prey to, after being chosen as God's people, was prejudice. Often in their prosperity they snubbed their noses at other nations, viewing themselves as being the only ones worthy of God's favor. In reality, it wasn't that they were so much better than other nations but that God's favor chose them for drawing other nations to repentance. Israel failed to see that God could have chosen any nation He wanted to but showed favor toward them to be His instrument to show the nations their sinful ways.

One of the most difficult things within the Body of Christ still today is looking beyond our cultural differences and seeing each other as spiritual brothers and sisters in Christ. I say this not to cause confusion and strife but to bring forth a reality that must be addressed if we are to be examples of Christ. Yes, we have more integrated churches than before, but just how integrated are we? Are we as integrated in our hearts as we are in appearance when we fellowship together? When we have a dispute with one another, does it emerge as one between brothers and sisters in Christ, or does a tinge of our national identity try to rise up?

In other words, do we handle our differences the same with everyone within the Body of Christ without prejudice or partiality? Because that's what prejudice is, showing partiality or favoritism for someone else, and it doesn't always involve race but can spring from a range of things.

One factor that has caused the birth of so many denominations and still does is doctrinal opinions. Doctrinal opinions, to me, are people's personal interpretation of God's word, which is usually closely connected with their feelings. A common practice of mine is to show a person what God's word says and let them read it for themselves. And if their understanding is still somewhat vague, I try to use more of God's word to broaden their understanding. But personal interpretation I try my best to consciously avoid.

The best I can do is to teach God's word with the help of His Spirit and pray for their understanding through those teachings. What I have learned as a teacher is that nothing reaches a person better than expressing God's word as it is written. All the eloquence of speech and clarity of words will never substitute for the written word. Yes, the Bible has been translated many times into different languages and formats for ease of reading, but I'm certain the meaning remains the same because it's still the inspired word of God that is spiritually interpreted by God—and God alone.

The best thing a teacher of God's word can do is encourage God's people to read and study God's word for themselves:

> Then the brethren immediately sent Paul and Silas away by night to Berea. When they arrived, they went into the synagogue of the Jews. These were more fair-minded than those in Thessalonica, in that they received the word with all readiness, and searched the Scriptures daily to find out whether these things were so. Therefore many of them believed, and also not a few of the Greeks, prominent women as well as men. (Acts 17:10–12 NKJV)

As Paul and Silas taught to those who had willing hearts to receive God's word, they not only received Paul and Silas's teachings but searched the scriptures to verify the truth in what they said. Everyone who is able within the Body of Christ has a responsibility to read and study God's word. How else will you know whether someone is teaching the truth?

So many souls have been misled by false doctrine simply out of a failure to read and study God's word themselves. Yes, we study and learn from other Spirit-led teachers, but their teachings can only go so far without our own personal reading of God's word.

If we truly understand our blood ties through Adam and Eve as God's creation, and now as born-again Christians, prejudice and any other form springing from it is not acceptable within the Body of Christ.

Collateral Damage

We have no idea of the cumulative damage done out of one act of disobedience. And probably we will never fully understand the consequences of Adam's willful act. The costly offense committed by Adam and Eve opened a Pandora's box of willful acts by humans beyond our imagination.

To this day we still have people questioning God's love whenever tragedy strikes, especially when it happens to those who we view as innocent victims. However, it's not a question of God's love as much as it is a matter of our acquired state resulting from Adam's disobedience.

Whether we acknowledge it or not, we all became collateral damage to sin through our inheritance of Adam's willful nature by disobeying God's will. Since the fall of Adam, every human being has been infected by the same sinful nature ushered in by one man's act of disobedience: "For as by one man's disobedience many were made sinners, so also by one Man's obedience many will be made righteous" (Romans 5:19 NKJV). We all have dwelling within our flesh that willful desire to make our own decisions absent of God's will.

One of the most heinous acts of hatred occurred within the first family of humankind. The murderous act of Cain against his brother Abel had nothing to do with God's lack of love for us but rather a lack of God's love being prevalent in man's heart as prior to his spiritual separation.

The damaging consequences of sin cannot be measured and should not be underestimated. Whenever we hear of, or experience something tragic, we should never attribute it to God but direct it to its origin, and that's Satan, who truly committed the first sin when he exalted himself before God. God's word clearly states His goodness and love toward us (Romans 5:8). The sinful things that occur in our lives are being committed by sinners and not orchestrated by God, because everything that comes from God is good: "Do not be deceived, my beloved brethren. Every good gift and every perfect gift is from above, and comes down from the Father of lights, with whom there is no variation or shadow of turning" (James 1:16–17 NKJV).

The merciless spirit that's been prevalent since the first act of sin by man is not of God but originates from Satan. If anything, God's grace and mercy have kept us from being consumed by our disobedience. Before

God created us, He made provisions for our sin by determining in Himself to become an offering for us as Jesus Christ. And it is God's grace and mercy that allows sin to remain. Not due to an insensitivity for our suffering but out of a desire to save us from sin's condemnation: "The Lord is not slack concerning His promise, as some count slackness, but is longsuffering toward us, not willing that any should perish but that all should come to repentance (2 Peter 3:9 NKJV)."

God is in the soul-saving business, and what some people consider slackness and indifference regarding the things being allowed to occur in the world is God's mercy withholding His judgment so souls will have an opportunity for salvation. If God were to destroy sin as many of us would like Him to, so would He have to destroy all of those who have not received Jesus Christ as their Savior. According to God's divine timetable, there will be a time when sin and the evils thereof will be destroyed, but not until God has redeemed all the souls Jesus Christ died for: "For God so loved the world that He gave His only begotten Son, that whoever believes in Him should not perish but have everlasting life. For God did not send His Son into the world to condemn the world, but that the world through Him might be saved" (John 3:16–17 NKJV). It's a choice that everyone must make, even though everyone will not choose Jesus Christ as their Savior. However, everyone will have an opportunity to do so, and God will not shorten that time until everyone has.

Yes, evil abounds with every passing generation, and will continue to do so with human existence, for it is not God Who is the culprit but humans who commit the sinful acts. And every sinful act carried out by humans can be linked to the first initial act of Adam's self-willed decision to disobey God's edict. Was Adam tempted? Yes, he was, as we all are in our daily lives. Even though God did not prevent Adam from being tempted in the Garden of Eden, Adam did not have to submit to his temptation but could have chosen to stand firm out of obedience to God's commandment.

From this, we've all become victims of consciously sinning against God's will:

> Therefore, just as through one man sin entered the world, and death through sin, and thus death spread to all men, because all sinned" (Romans 5:12 NKJV). Sin is in us, it's in our natural human DNA: "For I know that in me (that is, in my flesh) nothing good dwells; for to will is present with me, but how to perform what is good I do not find. For the good that I will to do, I do not do; but the evil I will not to do, that I practice. Now if I do what I will not to do, it is no longer I who do it, but sin that dwells in me. I find then a law, that evil is present with me, the one who wills to do good. For I delight in the law of God according to the inward man. But I

see another law in my members, warring against the law of my mind, and bringing me into captivity to the law of sin which is in my members. O wretched man that I am! Who will deliver me from this body of death? I thank God, through Jesus Christ our Lord! So then, with the mind I myself serve the law of God, but with the flesh the law of sin. (Romans 7:18–25 NKJV).

You can say those who don't belong to Christ truly have the "I can't help-its." For it is only by God's Holy Spirit that those of us who are in the Body of Christ are able to overcome our flesh and resist Satan's attacks against it.

Through our flesh we have been corrupted as well as crippled by its lustful desires whatever they may be. There are no limits to what we are capable of within our imaginations. Our only salvation from such collateral damage is God's Spirit. Without a spiritual rebirth of our spirit by God's Spirit, we'll never be able to develop into that spiritual family God designed us for. And after our spiritual rebirth, the issue of developing into a family of God remains. For I don't know about you, but as I look around, I sometimes wonder as members of the Body of Christ are we truly functioning as one body in Christ.

Coming Home

Before man's disobedience, there was perfect union between God and all His creation. But something drastically changed when humans disobeyed God's commandment not to eat from the tree of the knowledge of good and evil. First, let's look at Genesis 3:8–12. In verses 8–10, notice the immediate separation that has occurred between Adam and Eve and God. Rather than running to God, they're trying to hide from Him. Second, in verses 11–12 when God questions Adam about his disobedience, Adam turns on Eve and tries to pass the blame on to her. So now you have Adam and Eve not only having to deal with a fragmented relationship with God but with one another as well.

What has occurred is so vital in our existence with one another that until we come to terms with it, it's very unlikely that we will ever develop into the spiritual family God desires us to be. However, two scriptures I believe will help us better understand what happened between humans and God after their disobedience.

Let's look at Matthew 22:36–40 NKJV. After Jesus is asked about the great commandment, He replies: "You shall love the LORD your God with all your heart, with all your soul, and with all your mind. This is the first and great commandment. And the second is like it: You shall love your neighbor as yourself. On these two commandments hang all the Law and the Prophets." The same passage written in the gospel of Mark also states: "There is no other commandment greater than

My Brother's Keeper: A Servant's Heart

these" (Mark 12:31 NKJV). There is no commandment greater than these. And the total of God's law and the prophets hang on these two commandments, or, in other words, the word of God is encompassed by the principle of these two commandments. What principle, you might ask? Well, read on.

I've read these scriptures often, but one day the Lord blessed me to perceive them in a way I had never done before. The questions I believe God spoke into my mind started me thinking about what God was suggesting to us. I understood His telling us to love Him and each other. But as I began to explore deeper into the thought of loving God, I began to realize just how shallow my view of these scriptures was. God gave me a greater understanding on what He was expressing to us.

God is talking about something much deeper than a superficial or surface type of love. But a love that goes beyond emotions and feelings—one that penetrates the very core of our being. This love that God began to reveal to me is so intimate that nothing else matters without it. Understanding that until we learn to love God with everything we have in us, we will never be able to express love for anyone else including ourselves.

And then the critical question came, which I believe is the key to experiencing the intimate love that God desires to share with us. How can I learn to love God and people the way He desires me to? Then it was as though God opened the windows of heaven to my understanding, saying that in those scriptures He's

95

telling us to have a relationship with Him. The only way that we can develop the intimate love God is talking about is through an intimate relationship with Him. And that will only occur from sincere and regular interaction. It's only by our sincere desire to become close with God that we will ever experience the paternal love He has for us: "Draw near to God and He will draw near to you." (James 4:8 NKJV). So, the principle that God is conveying to us is that He desires for us to fall in love with Him and by doing so develop a relationship with Him, or as I like to call it, a love relationship.

Now let's journey back to the Garden of Eden where we left off with the dilemma that has developed between Adam and Eve and God. Of all the things resulting from their disobedience, the most detrimental of them becomes clearer as we consider Matthew 22:36–40, which reveals their damaged relationship with God and each other.

The first and foremost principle of God's great commandment is that above everything else we are to love and have a relationship with Him first. And second, like the first, is to love and have a relationship with one another. Somewhere between Eve eating from the tree of the knowledge of good and evil, and Adam doing the same, this principle of loving God first diminished. It seems that when Eve offered Adam the forbidden fruit, he placed his love for Eve above his love for God. There's no doubt that Adam loved him some Eve, so much so that he was willing to disobey God and die.

The edict God gave to Adam was crystal clear. There was no confusion on Adam's part. Now with Eve, scripture says something different. She was deceived; however, that did not excuse her act of disobedience as anything other than sin. They both sinned, but it seems the accountability weighed more on Adam than on Eve. I think about the parable told by Jesus regarding the faithful steward, and how he cautioned His disciples about accountability when He said: "And that servant who knew his master's will, and did not prepare himself or do according to his will, shall be beaten with many stripes. But he who did not know, yet committed things deserving of stripes, shall be beaten with few. For everyone to whom much is given, from him much will be required; and to whom much has been committed, of him they will ask the more" (Luke 12:47–48 NKJV).

In Eve's discussion with the serpent about the tree of the knowledge of good and evil, we see she wasn't completely clueless of her restriction from eating from it. But scripture says the serpent in some way cleverly enticed her into eating from the tree. *A life lesson can be learned from this; limit your conversation with those who oppose God's word.*

In Eve's conversation with Satan it seems as though he may have influenced her to misquote God's edict to Adam. Read Genesis 2:17 and Genesis 3:2–3, and you'll read where God commanded Adam not to eat of the forbidden tree, whereas Eve tells Satan she is not to eat of it or touch it. Now rest assured our adversary is very crafty at altering God's word to his advantage; all we must do is consider his attempts at tempting Jesus after His forty-day fast in the wilderness (Matthew 4:1–11).

Whatever may have occurred, I'm certain that Eve's addition to what God had said to Adam did not go unnoticed by Satan. And maybe, just maybe, he convinced Eve to touch the tree first, and seeing that she didn't die, Eve's own desire for the tree produced fertile ground for Satan to influence her to do what God had forbidden them to do—and that was eat from the tree of the knowledge of good and evil. Just a consideration, but one thing's for certain, and that is if Eve had stayed with God's commandment, whatever Satan said wouldn't have mattered. *Another life lesson: never consider anything outside or contrary to God's word.*

Scripture says Adam was not deceived: "And Adam was not deceived, but the woman being deceived, fell into transgression" (1 Timothy 2:14 NKJV). So, Eve fell into sin, but Adam boldly walked right into it.

Scripture strongly cautions us of willfully sinning against God's will.

> For if we sin willfully after we have received the knowledge of the truth, there no longer remains a sacrifice for sins, but a certain fearful expectation of judgment, and fiery indignation which will devour

the adversaries. Anyone who has rejected Moses' law dies without mercy on the testimony of two or three witnesses. Of how much worse punishment, do you suppose, will he be thought worthy who has trampled the Son of God underfoot, counted the blood of the covenant by which he was sanctified a common thing, and insulted the Spirit of grace? For we know Him who said, "Vengeance is Mine, I will repay," says the Lord. And again, *"The Lord will judge His people."* It is a fearful thing to fall into the hands of the living God. (Hebrews 10:26–31 NKJV)

To dispel any misconception of these above-mentioned scriptures of suggesting that God will destroy His people for willfully disobeying His word is not what is being said. The core of the message is the same as the message in Luke 12:47–48, which is to know God's will and not do it comes at a greater cost for someone than one who sins against God's word and didn't know it. Sin never goes unpunished; if it did, there would have been no need for Jesus's sacrifice on the cross.

So here we have Adam and Eve frightened, naked, and ashamed as they stood before God. They had their fig leaf, but to God they were totally bare in His sight. Their once perfect relationship with God shattered but, thank God, not destroyed. For even though grace as we know it hadn't manifested itself, it still was present with God as He dealt with their sin. If grace wasn't present, they wouldn't have been standing before God but lying dead before Him.

For God said with certainty that they would surely die if they were to violate the ordinance that He had forbidden them to disobey. But they were alive and yet dead in God's sight. Because the certain, or immediate, death God was speaking of was their spiritual death (separation from God spiritually), which did occur, and the subsequent natural death, which would come later. Thank God for His plan of salvation before our fall that His grace and mercy came forth at our fall.

Now what could be so persuasive that it would cause Adam and Eve to disobey God and risk dying? It seems so innocent, yet it can lead us into deadly consequences if not submitted to God's will. In the simplest term it's called desires, but when it turns deadly it can be called lusts. *Another life lesson: never allow your desires to rise above God's will.*

What transpired in the Garden of Eden with Adam and Eve can be a beacon of light for all of us. Mainly that God did not create us as robots but in His own image as beings with desires and the ability to make choices. Read Genesis carefully during God's creation process up to man's fall. God Himself said it is not good for man to be alone. Why? God created us as social creatures with a desire for companionship that was to gravitate toward Him and one another. Eve's desires for the forbidden tree were stirred by the serpent to entice her into sinning against God. Desires are not necessarily bad. They're part of our makeup. However, how we handle them determines the outcome for our lives. James warns us of uncontrolled desires:

> Blessed is the man who endures temptation; for when he has been approved, he will receive the crown of life which the Lord has promised to those who love Him. Let no one say when he is tempted, "I am tempted by God"; for God cannot be tempted by evil, nor does He Himself tempt anyone. But each one is tempted when he is drawn away by his own desires and enticed. Then, when desire has conceived, it gives birth to sin; and sin, when it is full-grown, brings forth death. (James 1:12–15 NKJV)

Desires are always with us. The question is how do we handle those that are contrary to God's will? Do we discipline them to God's will or entertain them until they grow beyond desires into that monster we know as lusts:

> For though we walk in the flesh, we do not war according to the flesh. For the weapons of our warfare are not carnal but mighty in God for pulling down strongholds, casting down arguments and every high thing that

> exalts itself against the knowledge of God, bringing every thought into captivity to the obedience of Christ, and being ready to punish all disobedience when your obedience is fulfilled (2 Corinthians 10:3–6 NKJV)

It's of our own volition when we toy with desires that we know are not God's will. And when our dwelling on them gives birth resulting into lust, we only have ourselves to blame when we sin by acting them out.

If you are wondering what all that I have said has to do with the question I asked earlier concerning our being so divided, believe me, I'm getting there. It's just that before you can construct a thought you need to build the foundation for it first. And that is what I'm trying to do for you as well as for myself.

You see, after our spiritual separation from God, one of the most catastrophic consequences was our dysfunctional behavior toward God. What was once normal became abnormal. This abnormality was not on God's part but ours. God still related to us; we just no longer possessed a healthy regard for Him. Remember that when God came to Adam and Eve after their disobedience, they hid themselves from God. Does that seem like normal behavior toward someone you have a loving relationship with? No, I think not.

The once perfect loving relationship had become shattered but not destroyed. For although man no longer gravitated toward God's love, God's care still reached out to us with His love (our brother's keeper). Our vision of God had become distorted as a natural man without spiritual life. Our natural self will never be able to relate to God properly. It's only by the spirit that God first breathed into us when we became a living soul (Genesis 2:7) that we will ever regain that spiritual channel of communication we once had with Him. As scripture tells us, fallen man must be born again. He must be born of the water and God's Spirit before any reunion with God can begin (John 3:3–6, Acts 2:38, Acts 4:11–12, Romans 8:9). It will take God's Holy Spirit to bring our dead spirit back to life to commune with Him and become that living soul we once were and be written in the Lamb's book of life for eternity.

So, why are we so divided as humans? Well, simply put, because of our falling out of relationship with God, we also fell out of relationship with each other. It's part of our nature. It's in our DNA. Our schisms are collateral damage from our fallen nature. We couldn't be of one accord if our lives depended on it. Oh, we might be able to do it for a "minute," but let someone do something we don't like, or suggest something we don't agree with, or let it be something we must follow from someone we regard as the tail when we feel that we are better suited to lead. Throw out the life preservers because war is imminent, and someone is about to be thrown overboard.

Sin became Pandora's box for our lives ushering in nothing but grief. And we've been straying further away from God and each other every step of the way. The monstrous and cruel acts we have committed against one another are true signs of our lack of affinity toward each other. There is no question as to our separation from one another. It's just a matter of how broad is the gulf that exists between us and how do we narrow it for our salvation with God and as a people.

I'm sure some of you know the answer, but for those who may not, our relationship with God must first be restored. And then we must look to God to show us through our renewed relationship with Him how to reestablish our relationship with one another.

Families Not Cliques

Coming back home to God is the only way back to building the family He calls for. God's commandment to His creation was to "be fruitful and multiply" (Genesis 1:22, 28). And from that commandment the many species of creatures and humankind increased. More importantly, families were born.

Humankind is made up of multiple nationalities and cultures. And it is families that make up nationalities, and people that make up families. No matter how large an individual family may be, it still derives its identity from its entirety—the extended family. At family reunions, you don't have families championing for which family is better (at least it shouldn't be), but its purpose is to restore and preserve family ties.

My family has been so blessed to have a family member who has dedicated many years of her life doing a genealogical study on our family. What she has accomplished has truly been a blessing for me, and I'm certain for so many other family members. From her efforts, God has not only blessed us with not one book but three filled with family history that has truly been inspiring. God bless you, Linda; we're so grateful for your love and commitment. Forgive me, readers, but I felt a need to take a moment to acknowledge God's blessings upon my family.

So, how do we go about restoring family ties as God's family, and after doing so, what can we do to preserve it? There's probably no one set pattern, but I believe there is a structure shown in the Bible that God gave to Israel for maintaining unity within the ranks of the people. And from this we could learn to build spiritual families making up the unified Body of Christ that God intended.

As mentioned before, this is not necessarily a blueprint but more so a foundation to build from. And an architect knows that the stability of any building lies within its foundation. If there's no strong foundation to build from, so goes the building that's built on it.

Seemingly one of the most common practices, or lack thereof, is our failure to see the value of consistent interaction with one another. Oh, we mingle with each other in church activities like Sunday school, Bible class, and weekly services. But is that sufficient for developing the kind of relationships needed to care for one another as brothers and sisters in Christ?

Are we purposely focusing on ways to develop sound avenues leading to building relationships within the Body of Christ? We not only should be doing this for the sake of growing closer but for survival as well. The sooner we grasp the reality that God never planned for us to experience life alone, the sooner we'll understand the value of relationships.

After man's creation one of the first things God addressed was man's inability to live alone: "And the Lord God said, 'It is not good that man should be alone; I will make him a helper comparable to him'" (Genesis 2:18 NKJV). We were designed to be dependent upon God, and codependent with each other:

> Two are better than one, because they have a good reward for their labor. For if they fall, one will lift up his companion. But woe to him who is alone when he falls, for he has no one to help him up. Again, if two lie down together, they will keep warm; but how can one be warm alone? Though one may be overpowered by another, two can withstand him. And a threefold cord is not quickly broken. (Ecclesiastes 4:9–12 NKJV)

God first created us for Himself and then purposely built within us a necessity for one another.

With that in mind, the question arises once again

as to how we restore and preserve the relationships and family ties God intended. Let's look at a familiar passage from the Old Testament regarding Moses's leadership of Israel in the wilderness (Exodus 18:13–26). Here we have Moses addressing the issues and concerns of God's people. In doing so, his father-in-law, Jethro, takes note of the tremendous responsibility Moses places upon himself. But Jethro also points out the great stress it causes among the people as well.

Moses's leading of God's people doesn't seem to be Jethro's concern. But how Moses is going about addressing the people's issues as their leader seems to draw great concern from Jethro. He lets Moses know that not only will his lone efforts to handle the people's issues wear him out but will wear out the people he is ministering to as well. This reality can serve well not just for pastors and leaders of God but for the Body of Christ as a whole.

First, it teaches pastors that even though God has given them the reigns as shepherd of His people, God does not expect them to tend to the flock by themselves. Second, it is the responsibility of leaders serving under the pastor to willingly share in the task of feeding and leading God's people. And third, it is the responsibility of the people to receive the leaders that the pastor has chosen to assist him. Therefore, it is so crucial that the pastor must first be in line with God so that those he teach will also learn how to serve as men and women of God.

The basis for choosing leaders expressed by Jethro is one that qualifies the person by how he lives along with his knowledge of God's law. Similar scriptures throughout the Bible express this practice as well. (Here are some that I commonly use: Acts 6:1–6, 1 Timothy 3:1–13, Titus 1:5–9, and 1 Peter 5:1–4). From these scriptures you can see the choosing of leaders and the role of leadership must be taken seriously. It has nothing to do with personal ties, popularity, or one's status but everything to with their quality of life lived before God. Before God grants anyone leadership over the lives of His people, you can be assured that He qualifies them first.

Now what does this have to do with building and preserving relationships and family ties with God and one another? Everything, because more often than not, with any family what the parents are like usually carries over to their children. So, to build small godly families that make up large godly families that make up larger godly families will necessitate godly leaders.

Along with qualifying God's leaders, the bodies within the Body of Christ (or the churches making up the Body of Christ) should be structured in a way that doesn't overburden any one person but extends the responsibility to other leaders. Note how Jethro's suggestion to Moses resembles what we come to know as immediate families making up the extended family.

The common immediate family today may make up five people (father, mother, and three children). And then the three children when they become grown may get married and have children, making up immediate families of their own. And their children may do the same, making up immediate families of their own, and so on and so forth, with all of them making up the family (or extended family).

And with that growth comes a greater responsibility; however, the great-grandfather or great-grandmother is not expected to personally address the needs of the great-grandchildren, nor the grandchildren, but their parents are. Yet being a godly example and influence for their children, their godly character is passed down, affecting the family as a whole. As the family (churches) of God, we should be structured similarly where the great and small concerns of the family are addressed.

As with any extended family, you have multiple families with multiple heads of household. And even though it's not as common today, there are still families that exercise a unified concern for the extended family by pooling their resources as multiple families for the common welfare of all who may have a need.

This is something that must be exercised within God's family. We are many members (families), but we make up one body, the Body of Christ. As a spiritual family, unlimited resources are available to us if we learn to share them communally and not hold onto them as personal possessions.

Now God doesn't expect anyone to do it all, no

matter how wealthy he or she is. Nor is it expected that those less fortunate should be excused from trying to do their part according to their ability. In other words, God doesn't expect anyone to do everything, but He does expect everyone to try and do something:

> For I do not mean that others should be eased and you burdened; but by an equality, that now at this time your abundance may supply their lack, that their abundance also may supply your lack, that there may be equality. As it is written, He who gathered much had nothing left over, and he who gathered little had no lack. (2 Corinthians 8:13–15 NKJV)

Just as in the world, the same exists in the Body of Christ; you have the wealthy along with the poor, and those that fit in between. And with a common interest for one another, we should be joining our efforts to address the needs of our spiritual family above our personal desires: "Now all who believed were together, and had all things in common, and sold their possessions and goods, and divided them among all, as anyone had need" (Acts 2:44–45 NKJV; read also Acts 11:27–30). And I'm certain this wasn't just for them but was written for our example to do the same.

I'm not suggesting that we start selling or giving away our possessions all willy-nilly but wisely. Just as one should be wise in planning to acquire wealth, he should be just as wise in planning how to distribute it to benefit others. You have many wealthy people within the Body of Christ as well as outside of it that have given billions to care for the needs of people. And I firmly believe that many of them are blessed of God to continue to make billions because of their pureness of heart to give. You see, I believe God can use the heart of anyone whether he or she is saved or not.

Finally, by structuring the Body of Christ this way (multiple leaders over multiple groups/families) we also offer one of the most important assets within a family—support groups. This is what immediate families offer within the extended family. Everyone needs that security blanket to comfort them in their life's journey. The extended family gives strength in numbers, but that inner circle (immediate family) gives one more of a sense of belonging and care.

It's not humanly possible to build strong intimate ties with everyone, but it is possible with a few. And a few is all you need for those exceptionally tough times in life. Jesus addressed and helped many, but He chose only twelve to have an intimate relationship with. With those twelve He shared things that He didn't even share with His parents and other close loved ones. And He did so not as a clique but as a spiritual family.

To this day you have some pastors who discourage and forbid forming groups within the church out of a fear of factions and cliques. And there are some pastors who have learned the value of encouraging support groups. I believe the key factor is what is being taught that supports the need for nuclear bodies within the Body of Christ. Are they being taught the mind-set of exclusivity or as an inclusive body making up the family of God? And whether you fight against it or not, people are going to form nuclear bodies, so leaders need to start teaching godly principals for developing them.

In our Christian journey, we all need someone we can place our confidence in. Not as God but as a friend. Remember God created us this way, not to go through life alone but together with Him as God in our lives. The extended family has a lot to offer, but in those times of needing a shoulder to lean on, someone to cry with, or those times when you need to share your frailties, you don't do that with just anyone but with those you feel closest to.

Neither do you bare your soul to the world but to a friend. And if you haven't learned by now, I'll tell you, if you have enough friends to count on one hand you are extremely blessed. Friends that stick closer than a brother. And yes, I know Jesus is that friend. But Jesus also purposed to bless us with friends that love us as He loves us: "A new commandment I give to you, that you love one another; as I have loved you, that you also love one another. By this all will know that you are My disciples, if you have love for one another" (John 13:34–35 NKJV). Yes, this scripture is for everyone who is in the Body of Christ, but wouldn't it be comforting to know that you have this kind of love with those you regard closest to you.

Finally, our immediate spiritual family (support group) offers what I believe to be one of the most crucial aspects of our spiritual walk with Jesus Christ, which is accountability. We all need someone we can place confidence in that will hold us accountable to how we live for Christ.

Those who we entrust with holding us accountable must also be faithful representatives of Jesus Christ themselves. Paul admonished those who followed him to do so as he exemplified Christ: "Be ye followers of me, even as I also am of Christ" (1 Corinthians 11:1 KJV). So, as mentioned before, we must also qualify those we bond with by how they model their lives with Christ: "Brethren, join in following my example, and note those who so walk, as you have us for a pattern" (Philippians 3:17 NKJV).

Who we associate with is paramount to our stability and faithful walk with Christ. If their lives do not reflect the life of Jesus Christ, if you're mature enough, help them to change. If you're not, move to higher ground with those who can help you grow and remain faithful to God.

Mainly we must realize that we are all related naturally, being creations by the same God through the fruitful reproduction of Adam and Eve. No matter how distant our bloodline may have become from the diversity of cultures and nationalities, if we as followers of Jesus Christ hold the word of God to be true, we are all genetically connected, for we're all offspring of Adam and Eve. And those who have received Jesus Christ as their Savior are now spiritually connected as brothers and sisters in Christ.

And as God's spiritual family, we are to live as an example for the world to see how God purposed us to live before our fall from grace. The family of God must model the family structure He ordained, one family at a time, within the Body of Christ. By this, as God's people, we will learn how to address the needs and concerns within the Body of Christ and become the channel that God called us to be for a dying world.

More Churches or Bigger Ones?

At best a church should be ministering to the community it's in, and the reality is that's where it will be most effective. No matter how large the church becomes, its tentacles will only reach so far because proximity is one of the factors for many people in determining what church they'll attend. You have some who will travel great distances to attend a church of preference; however, many of the worshippers usually are residents of the neighborhoods within the community.

So why do we build churches that outgrow the community as well as the people they're supposed to be ministering to? Are larger churches always better?

In an economics class I took in college, I recall the principle of "diminishing returns." Now this principle was used by many manufacturing companies to keep them from overproducing to avoid saturating the market with their product. This principle taught that every product has its point of nonproductivity. In other words, a point where demand for the product no longer satisfied its level of production, and to produce beyond that point would result in loses to the company rather than profits.

Every church whatever its size experiences attrition in some form or another. People leave one church for another for multiple reasons, but that's not my focus; my interest regards a common factor that develops with many larger church bodies. And that is what I call an "attrition of accountability." When Moses's father-in-law, Jethro, advised him of the danger of trying to counsel the people by himself, I believe one of his concerns was Moses's being able to monitor the people's accountability to God. This is important within any church body whatever the size. However, monitoring accountability becomes more challenging as the church body grows.

This is not an indictment against building larger churches, because sometimes it is necessary. But along with the larger facility, there is a mutual interest in developing a leadership that can and will address the needs of the people in the church. Is there a deliberate effort being made to structure the larger church as

Jethro advised Moses—to address the people, their concerns, their needs, and their accountability to God and one another? And this accountability to God and one another is the nucleus to any church body representing Jesus Christ.

Now accountability to God should be a no-brainer for anyone who belongs to Christ. The accountability to one another as followers of Jesus Christ may need a little explaining. What I'm suggesting is that we should be living our lives so exemplary to Christ's that it holds others accountable to do the same. This can serve as a barometer for both the leadership and the followers within the Body of Christ.

Leaders who understand their role as God's leader should know that they are held accountable for the care and safeguarding of the souls God has given them responsibility for: "Obey those who rule over you, and be submissive, for they watch out for your souls, as those who must give account. Let them do so with joy and not with grief, for that would be unprofitable for you" (Hebrews 13:17 NKJV). Throughout the Old Testament are accounts of how unfaithful leaders led to unfaithful followers.

We also have accounts of faithful followers of God being used by God to restore His leaders and people. This is something we mustn't take lightly as followers of Jesus Christ. Because as a church body within the Body of Christ, we often can leave our leaders vulnerable when we look to them as our example for strength, and not live as examples of Jesus Christ ourselves. Leaders, regardless of their maturity in Christ, still have weaknesses that can overcome them if they lack earthly support groups (humans within the Body of Christ) to draw from. Jesus Christ is the source, but He uses us as his examples to be tributaries to one another. More importantly, any example of Jesus Christ serves as an avenue for accountability to God.

With a seemingly concentrated interest in prosperity teaching and preaching, the desire for building larger and more lavish churches appears to be common practice among the more prominent pseudo leaders of today. We do have faithful leaders who have built larger churches purely out of a necessity to accommodate their services. But we also have some who have blended in as imposters, and some, sad to say, that belong to Christ that have fallen prey to greed and a lust for prominence and ego.

I won't concern myself with discussing the actions of those who do not know Christ but use religion as a cloak to satisfy their own personal desires. No, the focus is intended to be upon those leaders who belong to Christ and are building larger churches more out of a desire to increase membership for revenue purposes through tithes and offerings. Or as incredulous as it may sound, to have bragging rights of being a megachurch.

If you're increasing church membership and not the spiritual maturity of the people in it, what do you really have? It's likely that you have a lot of people who enable the church financially but who are not spiritually equipped to live for Christ. This can greatly affect a church's stability because anyone not rooted in the word of God is unlikely to practice the principles of it. And need I say that if your congregation consists mostly of unfaithful followers, however large the church body is, the paying of tithes and offerings is probably shaky as well.

You have pastors and board leaders who are very charismatic and more than qualified in structuring corporate churches that operate more like a business and are very successful at it. I personally don't believe that's God's intent but more so the leaders of that church. Being faithful stewards required those in leadership positions to be diligent and use sound judgment, as well as some business principles while carrying out the duties of a church's operations; however, not as a business for profit and gain but as an avenue to reach people for salvation through Jesus Christ. Cajoling people to sow into a ministry only goes so far and for so long.

My focus is not determining the reasons for building larger churches but to propose to God's faithful leaders the possible need to consider building more churches to better minister to the many communities on a broader and more personal scale. Now viewing this thought from the other side of the spectrum, we can certainly see there's no shortage of small churches either. As we travel through some neighborhoods, some could plead a case for an epidemic of small churches. I've seen in many instances where there may be several churches of the same faith in the span of one block. I call them splinter churches; some people address them as storefronts.

The thought I would like to convey is that oftentimes when we opt to build larger churches to reach more communities on a larger scale, we may better accomplish this by starting or building more moderate-size churches within that neighborhood or community. More often than not, larger churches have a surplus of qualified leaders to pastor churches. The problem arises quite often with a resistance to send them out with the support of the church God developed them in.

You have too many pastors today who are resistant to releasing qualified leaders who God has prepared under their tutorship for pastoring. Instead of realizing the privilege that God has granted them to take part in nurturing another soul for God's plan, they try to hold on to them for their own self-serving purposes. Parents who truly love their children take great comfort in seeing them grow into adulthood. And it brings them even greater joy knowing that they took part in that development.

The gratitude of sincere parenting is not to feel threatened from their children's growth but fulfilled. They look forward to when they'll be able to leave the nest in pursuit of their purpose in life. For another pastor to fail to see the value in releasing and supporting those God has used him to teach and prepare for the ministry is tragic. When God uses leaders to develop other leaders, they're not a threat to their ministry, but an asset to God's ministry, because every ministry of God belongs to God.

Apostle Paul took great interest in preparing leaders for shepherding churches God used him to start. This common practice during the early years of the New Testament church flourished I believe due to a commitment to increasing the Body of Christ instead of a fear of competing with one another. If more pastors had a mind-set of kingdom building rather than large church buildings, I believe the value of establishing manageable bodies within the Body of Christ would become more acceptable.

Reaching the world with the gospel of Jesus Christ is the commission for all of us who belong to Christ. And competing within the Body of Christ should not be our motivation for growth; our becoming one in Jesus Christ should be our inspiration for growth. The Body of Christ grows as our oneness with each other in Christ grows. Many members make up the Body of Christ, and no matter how large, no one member is its entirety. It is God that makes up the entirety; we're just members by His grace: "For in Him we live and move and have our being, as also some of your own poets have said, for we are also His offspring" (Acts 17:28 NKJV).

Leaders of God consider it an honor and privilege

when God uses you to prepare and support another ministry's growth. It takes a strong confidence in God to release devoted leaders as well as send faithful followers of Christ with them. But this is something leaders must learn to do out of a commitment to God's plan and purpose. Growth can come from attrition designed by God but never be the cause of attrition due to a lack of spiritual growth within the lives of those who are under your care. Losing members as laborers going out to increase God's harvest is not a loss but a gain for the kingdom of God. However, losing members due to an "attrition of accountability" because a church body has grown beyond managing the accountability of its members is truly a loss.

5

I AM MY BROTHER'S KEEPER

*"So which of these three do you
think was neighbor to him who
fell among the thieves?"*

(LUKE 10:36 NKJV)

Who is my neighbor? According to God's word, everyone is. It is spoken "to love thy neighbor as thy self" in three of the gospels (Matthew, Mark, and Luke) and a few other places in the New Testament. And whenever it is used, the word *neighbor* is used in the broadest sense, meaning to love your fellow human; in other words, any human. This is a vital part of the second-greatest commandment of God.

I think about a scripture passage that really hit home for me one day regarding how God wants us to love:

> You have heard that it was said, "You shall
> love your neighbor and hate your enemy."

But I say to you, love your enemies, bless those who curse you, do good to those who hate you, and pray for those who spitefully use you and persecute you, that you may be sons of your Father in heaven; for He makes His sun rise on the evil and on the good, and sends rain on the just and on the unjust ... Therefore you shall be perfect, just as your Father in heaven is perfect. (Matthew 5:43–45, 48 NKJV)

It took me a while to digest the gravity of what Jesus is saying to us, and in growing into this reality is a daily process for my life. For I face daily ordeals that challenge me to do otherwise.

When we learn to take this passage of scripture as is, we see there is no room for rejecting and hating anyone. No, we are required to treat everyone with love and kindness.

No Boundaries

As we reflect upon Matthew 5:43–45, 48, I believe what becomes most apparent to many of us is that this isn't something that will be easily done. How do we love our enemies? How do we bless those who curse us and be good to those who hate us? Just tell me, how do we find it in our hearts to pray for those who spitefully use and persecute us?

To get a better understanding of what was being asked of us, I looked up the words *spiteful* and *persecute*. And what I read sobered me even more to the charge that God gives us as His people. When someone does something spiteful against you, their intent is to deliberately harm you, and when it graduates to persecution, it is a persistent and continuous act of aggression to cause you distress. Now that's tough, but God expects it of us if we are to be called His children.

Let's look at Jesus's parable of the Samaritan in Luke 10:25–37. You often hear of this parable as the "Good Samaritan." Now Jesus doesn't speak of him as being good, but He does speak of his compassion.

This parable begins with a crime being committed against a traveler from Jerusalem on his way to Jericho. Note the two persons Jesus speaks of before He speaks of the Samaritan. A priest and a Levite (the assigned priesthood family of God), neither of them showing any concern or care for the wounded man. Now of all people, you would expect those who are called to be the oracles and representatives of God to show an interest in caring for someone in need. But they didn't. Does this resemble someone we may know? Before we answer, let us take a close look in the mirror.

So here comes the Samaritan, and Jesus says that when he saw the victim, he had compassion on him. Did not cross the road to avoid him, did not disregard his need for help; no, Jesus says he went to the injured man, which gives us the impression that the Samaritan purposely stopped to help the man. And then he not only had compassion for the wounded man; he showed compassion for him.

One of the first things I want to note is that as Jesus expresses what the Samaritan did, it seems to suggest that he would have done this for anyone. It didn't matter what nationality he was, whether he was rich or poor, or the color of his skin; all that seemed to matter was that he needed help. So, what I'm saying is that if we are to become the guardians God calls us to be, we must first learn not to regard anyone above another. God regards everyone, and so should we.

I don't care how much some may try to twist God's word to express Him showing more favor for those who are saved than for those who are not. I know a God that has "no respect of persons" but hung on the cross that "all might be saved" because of His love for all mankind (John 3:16–17). That's the God I know, and according to His word that's the God He will be until His final judgment of mankind when He opens the Lamb's Book of Life. If you can only help those who you feel merit your help, I assure you it's unlikely that you have the heart to consistently help anyone, whether they're inside the Body of Christ or not.

You see, we as human beings are notorious for establishing boundaries when it comes to helping someone, and it most often stems from an unwillingness to do so. We'd be amazed at how often people fail to help someone simply because they don't want to take the time. We have the resources and means and even can rearrange our time to be of help, but we just don't want to take the time to do it. And not taking time to do it is nothing more than a substitute for not wanting to do it. How sad.

However, the Samaritan interrupted his journey to stop and tend to a stranger's needs and then took the man along with him to continue caring for him as well as making provisions for his continued care. Note that he attended to the wounded man as long as he was with him, and when he had to leave, the Samaritan made arrangements for the injured man's care until his return. Did you get that? The Samaritan committed himself to being responsible for the wounded stranger's care, whether it was with his time, money, or his word.

Preferring One Another

The Samaritan not only stopped to attend to the stranger, but he also disregarded his safety for the sake of assuring the stranger's safety. From the parable it seems the road taken from Jerusalem to Jericho was not a safe one. Knowing this, it is unlikely that anyone would feel safe traveling alone, much less stopping to help someone no matter what the situation may be.

What the Samaritan did is nothing we should take lightly. He placed himself in harm's way by stopping to attend to the man's wounds. But now he places himself in greater danger by placing the man on his animal

(more than likely a donkey) to carry him along, which slows him down because he probably now must walk to keep from overburdening the animal. Walking was a common mode of traveling then, and to have an animal to ride was a luxury. So now here we have a man who is probably well off financially, willing to jeopardize his safety to save the life of a stranger.

When I think about this Samaritan's willingness to place himself in harm's way to help someone, I think about a particular scripture: "Be kindly affectionate to one another with brotherly love, in honor giving preference to one another" (Romans 12:10 NKJV). This preference for one another is the same as one esteeming someone else's life so much so that they don't value their life or interests more than another's life. Even to the point of jeopardizing their welfare to assure someone else's. Not that they don't value their own well-being, but that they equally value someone else's life as their own.

Jesus loved us to the point of giving up everything, including His life, for our benefit. And Jesus expects the same from us:

> By this we know love, because He laid down His life for us. And we also ought to lay down our lives for the brethren. But whoever has this world's goods, and sees his brother in need, and shuts up his heart from him, how does the love of God abide in him? My little children, let us not love in

word or in tongue, but in deed and in truth. And by this we know that we are of the truth, and shall assure our hearts before Him (1 John 3:16–19 NKJV)

Laying down our lives for others involves everything about us as well as our possessions.

Jesus gives us access to everything about Him and everything He owns. So, if you believe that what you have you truly own, let me enlighten you to the reality that what you so call own has really been consigned to you from the One Who owns everything. And for those who may not know Who I'm talking about, His name is Jesus Christ. All Jesus must do is blow on what you treat as yours and place you in the same condition as those you refuse to help.

God never intended for us to hoard our earthly possessions but to use them for His glory by helping others. If we are to do any storing of our treasures, it should be in heaven where we are to spend eternity: "Do not lay up for yourselves treasures on earth, where moth and rust destroy and where thieves break in and steal; but lay up for yourselves treasures in heaven, where neither moth nor rust destroys and where thieves do not break in and steal. For where your treasure is, there your heart will be also" (Matthew 6:19–21 NKJV). Many of us hold unto our possessions as though this is going to be our permanent place of residence. People of God, this should not be the case within the Body of Christ.

I have yet to see nor hear of anyone who has died and taken their earthly possessions with them where it has done them any good after their death. We place way too much value in our possessions and too little value in the lives that can benefit from them. I believe the more treasures we hoard for ourselves here on earth, the less we store for ourselves in heaven: "He who has pity on the poor lends to the Lord, and He will pay back what he has given" (Proverbs 19:17 NKJV). If this scripture doesn't stir you to sharing your earthly goods, what more can I say that will?

I think of the rich man who asked Jesus what he had to do to have eternal life (Matthew 19:16–22, Mark 10:17–22). And after Jesus told him to sell his possessions to give to the poor, the rich man went away sad and sorrowful. One of the saddest parts of this passage is that when Jesus told the rich man that by doing so, he would have treasure in heaven, and that apparently had little value to him versus his riches on earth. How many of us have similar mind-sets regarding our possessions? By placing greater value in our worldly goods than heavenly ones?

Do we consider that when we withhold our resources from the poor, we're withholding them from God as well? Please revisit Proverbs 19:17. And not only that, but we could very well be cursing our life by our insensitivity to those in need: "He who gives to the poor will not lack, but he who hides his eyes will have many curses" (Proverbs 28:27 NKJV). We harp more and more about how we want to be like Jesus but refuse to live like Him. We need to stop sounding like we care and start showing it. If I'm hungry, your words will do nothing for filling my stomach, but if you purchase me something to eat, your words just may have some meaning as my hunger diminishes.

Sharing the Wealth

Our willingness to share with others is a direct reflection of where our heart is with God. From a godly perspective, it has always been the responsibility of the prosperous to share their wealth with those less fortunate. This was one of the edicts that God gave to Israel: "When you reap the harvest of your land, you shall not wholly reap the corners of your field, nor shall you gather the gleanings of your harvest. And you shall not glean your vineyard, nor shall you gather every grape of your vineyard; you shall leave them for the poor and the stranger: I am the Lord your God (Leviticus 19:9–10 NKJV; also read Deuteronomy 24:19–22).

Now how would such an edict apply today? Whatever their harvest, God commanded Israel to allot some of it to make provisions for those in need. Undoubtedly most of what they harvested was purposed for securing their welfare whether it was done by marketing, trading, or accumulation. However, it was not to be done in such a way as to disregard the needs of others.

As we plan and work for our necessities in life, do we have the welfare of others in mind? Do we purposely set aside some of our resources to assist someone in need if the time arises? Or do we regard providing for those less fortunate as secondary to our welfare? Many scriptures caution us about considering ourselves above others. I would like to use two scriptures to support this thought. Keep in mind that there are other scriptures that can build on the two that I am about to discuss. And if we read and study God's word as we should (Acts 17:11, 2 Timothy 2:15), we'll find them. And when we do, it will be a simple matter of being willing to obey them.

> Jesus said to him, "You shall love the Lord your God with all your heart, with all your soul, and with all your mind." This is the first and great commandment. And the second is like it: "You shall love your neighbor as yourself." On these two commandments hang all the Law and the Prophets. (Matthew 22:37–40 NKJV) (Mark 12:31)

> Be kindly affectionate to one another with brotherly love, in honor giving preference to one another. (Romans 12:10 NKJV)

The first and great commitment is to love God, and the second great commitment is like the first—to love your fellow man as you would love yourself.

This neighbor Jesus is speaking of is not exclusive to those within the Body of Christ but inclusive of the human race as mentioned earlier. Although sadly some of us have difficulty being neighborly toward one another as brothers and sisters in Christ. And we wonder why we can't broaden our horizons outside the Body of Christ.

Loving someone else as yourself is quite clear and yet very challenging. When we seriously consider what is being said, we can't disregard the welfare of others while regarding our own well-being. If I truly love myself, I certainly want what's best for me. And if I love you as myself, then I also want what's best for you.

I often read Romans 12:10 in hopes of getting a better understanding with every reading of what God meant by preferring one another. And I believe what we are to do is not so much to disregard our needs while trying to meet the needs of others. But we are to regard others in such a way as to strive for their welfare the same as we would our own. It's like a story I once heard about a person having a meal. It wasn't much, but it was better than nothing. Now the dilemma was that he wasn't the only one who needed food. He had a friend who was hungry also. So, he had to choose between satisfying his hunger or sharing what he had. The moral of the story was that he shared what he had with his friend with the understanding that although he wouldn't go to bed with a full stomach, it was better that neither of them went to bed hungry.

This is how we should go about our lives in sharing what we have with those less fortunate so they will have something, instead of hoarding what we have leaving them with nothing. If we truly consider these scriptures as God purposes us to, how can we not allot some of our resources for those in need, the same as we do for ourselves? What will it take for us to gain the determination to say no to things we want so that we can say yes to things people need. God knows, and I pray that as He shows us, we willingly submit.

To love someone as myself and prefer their well-being is not placing their needs above my own, nor is it placing my needs above theirs but equally placing value in their life as I would my own. As you ponder this kind of love, read 1 Corinthians chapter 13, Galatians 5:13–26, and Colossians 3:12–17. I'm giving you these scriptures as a tool in hopes of you better understanding the difference in being self-serving and serving. There are many other scriptures that distinguish the differences; you just must desire to know them.

No Free Rides

Out of this giving also comes accountability for the recipients of this care. It has never been God's intention for anyone to live freely from someone else's labor. One of God's first edicts to Adam and Eve in the Garden of Eden was to "be fruitful and multiply" (Genesis

1:27–28). In other words, be productive. And that has not changed. God affords no one the attitude that things should be given to them with no effort on their part for receiving it.

God's word states: "In all labor there is profit, but idle chatter leads only to poverty" (Proverbs 14:23 NKJV). Being productive is good for everyone no matter how rich or poor you may be. Are there ever occasions where someone has need of free gifts? Of course there are. Jesus said that we will always have the poor among us. However, that doesn't excuse anyone from having a desire to provide for themself if they are able.

No one should give in such a way as to foster laziness in those they are trying to help. In one of Paul's letters to the Thessalonian church he says: "For even when we were with you, we commanded you this: If anyone will not work, neither shall he eat" (2 Thessalonians 3:10 NKJV). Paul not only preached this belief but practiced it as well (2 Thessalonians 3:7–9). Please read (2 Thessalonians 3:6–13) to better understand that Paul is not promoting a spirit of not sharing but of having a good conscience of honest living among each other.

As it was in Paul's time, and before, and even now, you have those who will take advantage of those who give freely. But don't allow that to clog your heart from giving. Just move on and keep sharing. Don't let someone's exploits of your kindness set you up for missing your blessings. You never know who you might be serving (Hebrews 13:1–2).

To withhold from those in need can be risky and detrimental. The conniving of one person can set you up to be insensitive to someone who truly is in need. And that can be displeasing to God, which is never a good thing: "Whoever shuts his ears to the cry of the poor will also cry himself and not be heard" (Proverbs 21:13 NKJV).

Come to an understanding that to truly give freely you must be willing to be vulnerable to being taken advantage of. Read Matthews 5:43–48 again along with 2 Corinthians 5:12–21, emphasis on verse 17). It comes with the territory of being a loving new creation of God with your salvation. Read and study these scriptures carefully for they are not easily digested. It will take a lot of crucifying the flesh to receive the spirit of what is being said.

I've read Matthew 5:43–48 often to keep myself grounded to what God desires of me as His vessel. But one thing is certain every time I read it. I'm reminded of what Jesus Christ did for my salvation. And if you take it personally like I do, you're thinking the same.

It's not easy being used, even when you know it's God's will. But there's no getting around it if we truly understand God's call for our lives (1 Peter 2:18–21). Now to those who look for opportunities to use people's generosity for their advantage, a word of caution: "Wealth gained by dishonesty will be diminished, but he who gathers by labor will increase" (Proverbs 13:11 NKJV).

If dishonest gain comes at a cost for the wealthy, at what cost does it come for the poor? Don't let the look of prosperity deceive you into thinking that dishonest gain is unchecked by God. I assure you that those who have enjoyed the luxuries of wealth through dishonest gain will be held accountable. And whether now or at the judgment seat of Jesus Christ, they will gladly surrender all they have for the peace of God that they abandoned.

Taking advantage of people who are trying to help you doesn't hurt them as much as it destroys you. It's like a drug lulling you into a deep sleep of laziness: "Laziness casts one into a deep sleep, and an idle person will suffer hunger" (Proverbs 19:15 NKJV). You begin to waste away as your slothful ways consume you: "The desire of the lazy man kills him, for his hands refuse to labor" (Proverbs 21:25 NKJV). Don't be like some who look for handouts instead of opportunities to provide for themselves.

Whatever your desires are, it accomplishes nothing without diligence. Having things given to you doesn't fulfill you as a person. Neither does instant wealth (Proverbs 23:4–5). Never go through life with the attitude of getting something for nothing. It will only impoverish your soul instead of prosper it: "The soul of a lazy man desires, and has nothing; but the soul of the diligent shall be made rich" (Proverbs 13:4 NKJV). A rich soul far surpasses all the wealth in the world. For those who may be in need, whatever it may be, I pray for you as John prayed: "Beloved, I pray that you may prosper in all things and be in health, just as your soul prospers" (3 John:2 NKJV).

6

WHAT DOES IT TAKE?

*Strengthening the souls of the disciples,
exhorting them to continue in the faith,
and saying, we must through many
tribulations enter the kingdom of God.*

(ACTS 14:22 NKJV)

It takes kingdom builders to build a kingdom, and as God's church we're all called to be kingdom builders. And being God's church makes us a part of His kingdom. So along with our call to leading souls to Christ, we're also called to build up each other's lives (Ephesians 4:11–16).

This will take sacrifice and commitment on our part to be our brother's keeper. To have the mind-set of genuinely giving oneself purely for the sake of others is more than a notion (Philippians 1:23–25). How many of us are willing to accept the bonds of suffering for someone else's sake? (2 Timothy 2:10).

To endure the sacrifices necessary to fulfill the call of a "brother's keeper" must reach beyond our superficial feelings. Caring for someone unselfishly takes a profound passion powered and orchestrated by God's Holy Spirit. What does it take?

No Fanfare/Plenty Reward

I think about a time when a young man shared with me a trying time in his life when he experienced a life-threatening illness. He told me how he had been involved in a men's ministry for years. And during that time, how he had participated in prayer groups, Bible studies, feeding homeless men, and many other activities to show their care for men in general.

However, when a serious illness surfaced in his life, those same brothers he earnestly served with showed very little concern for him in his time of need. When he reached out to share his illness with a few brothers he felt closest to, he got little response.

This was heart-wrenching to say the least to this young man. But even more disturbing was that during his extended absence, not one brother came to visit him. He thought that even though he hadn't shared his condition with any of them, at least by his absence someone would have taken an interest to visit him. He said he had gotten a few token phone calls. However, he felt that was a poor substitute for men he had not only served with while ministering to others but some he had personally ministered to in their time of need.

As he continued, I sensed a deep hurt not so much out of bitterness but disappointment. After ministering so faithfully with brothers he had come to love so dearly, only to find out their love wasn't as genuine as it appeared.

I thought, how often have we superficially projected the image of caring if it was convenient? If we can do so without having to go out of our way, everything is fine. But don't expect me to make any sacrifices or inconvenience myself to show that I care.

I've seen and experienced within God's church people serving in the ministry and failing to minister to one another. If we fail to minister within the Body of Christ, just how effective are we to those outside of it? Do we not see the collective damage we cause when we fail to minister to those we minister with?

I remember a time when I was suffering a serious drought in my life. I mean years of going through a period dealing with ungrateful and insensitive people. So much so that I had become seriously displeased with God's handling of my situations and suffering. Yes, I'm willing to admit that there have been times when I got upset with God. Not the wisest of things to do, I admit, but along with my ignorance I learned valuable lessons about God's grace. Mainly that many times in my ignorance God's love provided His grace to keep me with His mercy.

There was a time that I had gotten so upset that I shared with a pastor friend my disappointment of not having someone to care for me in my time of need. I told him I didn't understand why God was allowing me to suffer and experience so much indifference by those I thought cared for me. It seemed the more God placed me in the position to help someone, the more apathy I experienced from others regarding my need.

These hurtful experiences were coming at me so frequently that I found myself unconsciously warring against bitterness and resentment. I say unconsciously because initially I hadn't realized how I was developing some resentment toward some of the people I loved. I was addressing it as righteous anger due to their insensitivity for what I was going through. But it was teetering heavily toward bitterness.

After wearing myself out trying to find an answer everywhere else, God blessed me to have enough sense to finally address my issues with the only One Who had the answer. I began fervently asking God why He wasn't providing genuinely caring people in my time of need, as He had used me to care for others.

My agony grew that much more when I didn't get an immediate answer. In fact, it took some years before God increased my understanding with His response to my question. I assure you God's answer was very humbling and reassuring. God spoke to my heart saying, "because you asked for it." This blew my mind, but as I pondered what was said, God brought to my remembrance something I had prayed for years ago. I had asked God to teach me how to love and be more like Jesus Christ. Oh, the jubilation I felt when God revealed to me what was going on in my life.

Has it been easy since? Not for my flesh, but my spirit has grown phenomenally. God has used my disappointments to teach me that to be and love like Jesus Christ, I must learn to love and care for those who may not do the same for me. And that has truly been a blessing. It hasn't always been easy, but the liberty given me by releasing the weights of hurt and resentment has been spiritually therapeutic. Without this ability to love unselfishly, it's unlikely we'll ever be able to minister in the trenches of God's kingdom.

God spoke to my heart, saying that He still wanted me to love, care, and be there for them. Why? So they can see what His love is like. This call is for all who belong to Jesus Christ: to shine as "the light of the world" as He did while He was in the world. And nothing shines greater than God's love. If you're looking for praise and applause, God's ministry isn't for you. And yet God's ministry is mandated for all who are His.

Change of Venue/Nothing Personal

Walking the pathway of selfless living is very demanding. And trying to travel it regarding one's self before and above the lives of others only hinders it. Our journey must be traveled with an attitude of equally regarding other people's lives as our own. The demands placed upon our lives in doing so is trying enough without the added burden of dealing with relationships that hinder us from going forth in God's purpose.

One of the most difficult challenges in life can be severing old ties for new ones. I did not say severing friendships, although that may be the result sometimes. As hurtful as it may be, there may be times when we must move away from people who are close to us to be more productive in our commitment to God's call.

There was a time in my life when a persistent thought kept cropping up in my mind (heart) crying out, "kindred spirits." A little while after that, I began feeling this strong desire to have some quality quiet time with God (a sabbatical of sorts). During this period, I would meditate more on this cry of "kindred spirits" when I prayed. Eventually God revealed to me that what He wanted me to do was to start seeking people with similar passions as mine for the ministry.

I didn't take to this right away but continued trying to travel the road I had grown accustomed to in supporting the ministries I was involved with. You see, it took me a while to realize that even though every ministry is supposed to be leading souls to Christ, everyone may not have the same vision. We should all have a passion for drawing souls to Christ, but our vision for the souls we reach out to may be different. Some may have visions that give them a passion for reaching out to seniors, some to the incarcerated, and others to the homeless, whereas some may be as broad as helping people in general.

In the early beginnings of the New Testament church, many of the apostles' ministries concentrated on reaching the Jews, whereas Paul's ministry was to the Gentiles. But all their ministries were about leading souls to Jesus Christ. While fulfilling their call to the ministry, they addressed the different needs of the people along with their designed purpose and passion from God.

As our vision becomes clearer, we may find ourselves taking different paths than the people we are close to, and that can be very difficult. Separation of any kind is not easy. But we must always stay mindful that it's not about our plans but about God's purpose. And sometimes God's purpose is not going to mesh with our desires, but we can take comfort in God's will always being best for us.

There may also be times when we must sever ties simply because some people are not fruitful for our lives even though they are close to our hearts. Have you ever experienced relationships where it seems as though you're never the recipient but always the giver? And even those times when something seemingly comes your way, you're the one that's drained most of the time from the relationship. They're drawing from you, but it seems you rarely can draw from them for strength.

It's like trying to charge a battery with dead cells. All it does is keep drawing from the charged battery but never holding a charge, and before you know it, the charged battery is dead as well. Some people are like that. They'll draw from your life but seldom if ever can you draw from theirs. And before you know it, you're drained of your strength.

I'm not suggesting that we shouldn't allow people to draw from our lives. We've all done it before and will have to do it again. But if you find yourself always being the spark plug not having someone close to get charged from, you may need to change your surroundings.

There should be times when you can draw from a friend also, if it truly is a friendship: "As iron sharpens iron, so a man sharpens the countenance of his friend" (Proverbs 27:17 NKJV). If you're the only one doing the sharpening, your spiritual life is in jeopardy, and the sharpness in your life is soon to dull. Don't allow people to paint you as their strength where you never grow weary. There's only one Person that fills that role, and that is Jesus Christ. No, we all need someone for support during our journey.

I've learned that not everyone is purposed for your immediate family (inner circle) I spoke of earlier. And I know some pastors are uncomfortable with the thought of people having a select group they may prefer bonding with. But whether you accept it or not, it's being done and will continue to be done. It's common practice for people to gravitate to those they feel something in common with. So why not teach them how to do it as the Body of Christ.

Families are made up of smaller families and so is the Body of Christ: "For as the body is one and has many members, but all the members of that one body, being many, are one body, so also is Christ. For by one Spirit we were all baptized into one body, whether Jews or Greeks, whether slaves of free, and have all been made to drink into one Spirit. For in fact the body is not one member but many" (1 Corinthians 12:12–14 NKJV). I love my natural and spiritual family, and yet there are only a select few that I am willing to share personal things with. Not necessarily out of distrust but from a sense of closeness with the select few. We all need that inner family for security and support. We just need to learn how to do it according to God's word.

Plants and trees need pruning for growth, and there may be times when we need pruning within our inner family to promote growth in our lives. Whatever the reason may be and however close we may be to that person, we should not resist the needed change. Paul and Barnabas separated over an issue Paul had with John Mark. And I'm certain it wasn't easy, but they did what they had to do. It may not be as controversial as Paul and Barnabas's was but simply out of necessity. This separation doesn't mean that the person you're moving from is bad for you; you're just traveling a different path. You're both going in the same direction (fulfilling God's will) just using a different road to get there.

Choose Wisely

Jesus Christ chose His inner family and with the guidance of the Holy Spirit he expects us to take part in forming our inner family. In doing so, we can't allow feelings to interfere with sound judgment. Basing choices with our feelings is usually more superficial than anything. This can lead to poor choices because our feelings are too closely related to our emotions. And for those who may not know (or admit) it, emotions are like a rollercoaster; they're up and down. Uncontrolled, they can affect our feelings, making them very unreliable.

When considering someone a friend, it's usually more from what we feel for them than what they do for us. So, when I call someone my friend, it's more out of how I show it with my actions toward them. Proverbs 18:24 (NKJV) reads: "A man who has friends must himself be friendly, but there is a friend who sticks closer than a brother." This scripture is stating the value of close relationships, especially with God and then with others. But it's also cautioning us of having too many friends.

The word *friend* in the first portion of the verse (according to the *Hebrew-Greek Word Study Bible*) is used in the broadest sense, which can range from a close loved one, acquaintance, or adversary. Whereas friend in the second portion of verse 24 expresses a deep love and affection as toward a lover or close loved one. Also, some Greek texts differ where it reads "must show himself friendly" (but read "may come to ruin" or "comes to ruin").

From this verse we can learn a lot about limiting our close relationships. However, a few considerations, I believe, are worth noting. One is when we try to associate ourselves with a lot of people, we spread ourselves thin for giving quality time for genuine relationships. To develop sincere friendships takes time and effort. And if we give of ourselves as true and loving relationships require, it can be consuming if not managed properly.

All friendships are trying at times. And can be demanding as we learn to endure each other and one another's burdens: "A friend loves at all times, and a brother is born for adversity" (Proverbs 17:17 NKJV). However, friendships should never sap the life out of those involved but should nurture healthy bonds. No matter how loving you are, you can only give so much of yourself before your energy begin to wane. Jesus Christ (God in the flesh) only chose twelve as close friends, and one of them betrayed Him.

Which brings me to my second point, and that is along with overextending ourselves with a broad friend base also lurks the danger of superficial friends. Superficial relationships are mostly limited to emotions and are very limited in what we are willing to give of ourselves. The bond that penetrates beyond our feelings inspires us to do things we wouldn't normally do. The broader the friend base, the greater the possibility for this happening.

Having a friend that sticks closer than a brother shouldn't ever be taken lightly. If you should find one in a lifetime, consider yourself blessed. A person you can pour the very depths of your soul out to. Not having a concern for vulnerability but an unswerving confidence of loving care and security.

Everyone needs someone they can bare themselves to without fear of mistrust. Trust is something every person needs for establishing close ties. Every relationship will have its disappointments. However, no relationship should weigh a friendship down with the expectations of a friend never disappointing the other. That's not possible.

Jesus Christ entrusted things with his twelve disciples that He didn't with others. And one of the twelve betrayed that trust. In life we're going to be disappointed and even possibly betrayed by someone we considered close to us, which deems it necessary to take extreme care in choosing those we develop friendships with. Our inner family should be close and spiritually knitted together. For it is no stronger than the spiritual bond within it. Most importantly, this spiritual bond must be empowered by God's Holy Spirit. The broader your friend base becomes, the less of a nucleus your inner family becomes as well.

Jesus Christ understood this reality well. And even though the human side of Jesus suffered many disappointments from His disciples, His divine side knew He would be able to trust them after His resurrection. Now if Jesus being Who He is confined His inner family to a limited number during His earthly stay, who are we to attempt anything differently with our human frailties. Jesus Christ had many disciples (followers), but as a human being He kept His close relationships to a minimum.

Everyone needs that special bond that goes beyond family ties. Someone who will be there at all costs if need be. A relationship where one's welcome never wears out. Where there are no boundaries when it comes to showing their love. Friends like that are few. It's not easy building relationships of this nature or preserving them. That is why we must take special care in not trying to build too many. Committed relationships are time consuming, requiring a lot of personal involvement. Who we select for our inner family is vital for our accountability and spiritual growth, as well as for our replenishing after being exhausted from everyday living. So, choose wisely those with whom you entrust your confidence. God never intended for us to walk our journey alone, but He does expect us to be careful of those we choose to walk with.

7

A FINAL WORD

*He who has a generous eye will be blessed,
for he gives of his bread to the poor.*

(PROVERBS 22:9 NKJV)

Being your brother's keeper isn't always easy. However, it is something God calls us to do. You're going to have to do phenomenal things from a natural viewpoint yet the norm from a godly standpoint. Phenomenal because with the natural eye it would seem foolish doing those things necessary to enrich someone else's life; nevertheless, the godly thing to do because God requires it. And when you think about it, whatever we find ourselves doing for someone else Jesus Christ has already done for us as our earthly example.

We will always have the poor and wealthy on this earth. Not due to God's design but from man's sinful greed. Not to say that everyone that's wealthy did so dishonestly. But I will say that personal wealth was not meant for selfish gain but for communal support.

If you're the only one benefitting from your fortune, you're not heeding God's word in giving. Scripture upon scripture commands communal charity for those in need. And that giving goes far beyond one's immediate family or inner circle. It encompasses wherever there is a need.

There's no better place for this type of giving to be exemplified than within the Body of Christ. Not to say that the church is responsible for resolving the social ills of the world. However, the individuals who are able that make up God's church do have a responsibility to address people's needs.

For those who continue to struggle with accepting God's word on giving, I pray for God's grace to deliver you. Most often it's just a matter of trusting God with our resources to free us up for giving. Don't be begrudging like the rich ruler (Matthew 19:16–22) who could not see God's blessings in sharing his wealth.

Sadly, many will have difficulty receiving the message of this book. Not necessarily because they're unwilling but more from a limited knowledge and understanding of God's word. I'm amazed at the number of God's people I know who have a pretty good knowledge of God's word but have never completely read the Bible.

The Bible clearly states that it is our responsibility to read and study it (2 Timothy 2:15). Why? For understanding—having knowledge of God's word without understanding does little for our being able to apply it. I've known well-educated saints of God who express the letter of God's word wonderfully and fail miserably at applying the spirit of God's word. For example, some still try to live the law of God's word and fail to see the significance of applying God's grace. They fail to see it's the grace of God's word that grants us salvation and not the law (Ephesians 2:8–9).

To understand any other writings regarding the word of God, you had better first seek an understanding of God's word by reading it. It is by God's word that we determine the truth of whatever else we may read. Many inspired writers led by God help us develop a fuller understanding of God's word. But we should never substitute their writings for God's word.

There is something I have been doing since my salvation, and I thank God for placing it in my spirit. I'm not saying this to boast but to express the importance of reading God's word on a regular basis. What I do is read the Bible from Genesis to Revelations continuously. Whatever I may be studying in the Bible, or inspirational book I may be reading, along with it I'm also reading the Bible from beginning to end continually.

How many times I have read the Bible is not important to me, so I haven't kept count. What is important is that I'm always reading God's word for a fuller understanding. And that's my encouragement to everyone—to read all of God's word—and I assure you with each reading God will increase your understanding. Stop depending on someone else to study for you. We should all have something to offer when sharing God's word. Some may have more to offer than others, but no one belonging to God should be void of understanding some of God's word.

Understanding God's word is instrumental in receiving the teachings of His word by others. It also serves as a safeguard from being deceived by false teachings. So, if you have trouble with what I have written in this book, I'd rather it be from your lack of knowledge and understanding due to not reading the Bible than from an unwillingness to accept it out of an insensitive heart to God's word and people's welfare. I'm confident that what I have written is inspired by God because it is based upon the scriptures written in His word.

As we learn to give more freely, we also will be more vulnerable to being used. Just as we will always have the poor among us, we'll also have those who will take advantage of our kindness. But don't allow that to discourage your giving (Galatians 6:9–10). Don't let someone's treachery affect your commitment to pleasing God. And please don't allow a few bad apples to have you start trying to discern who you should and should not be charitable to. It'll only trip you up into giving less instead of more.

To keep me on course, I take God's word literally for

understanding. I don't try to govern it mixed with my interpretation. So, when God's word tells me to turn no one away in my giving (Luke 6:30–31), who am I to question? I should not allow my concern as to how they will use it to interfere with my desire to help them.

I've heard so many angles on determining who and who not to give to. Giving from that perspective is too taxing for me. So, I concluded I'd rather misstep trying to live God's word than misstep from not trying. I try to give freely to everyone that asks whether it's monetary or some other means of giving.

Some of you may say, "but I can't afford to give what people ask of me." It's not so much the amount you give of your resources, time, or yourself. It's the spirit you have in your giving. Since money is a problem many of us have when it comes to giving, let me give an example of giving with a purpose. As limited as some of our resources may be, how many of us deliberately set aside and divide some of our money in low enough denominations to try and give something to as many people as possible that solicit our help. I'm talking about money we have specifically set aside and replenish to have something to give whenever someone ask us for assistance.

Whatever they may be asking for, do you try to give them something? They may ask for a dollar, and all you have is ten dollars for the week. Are you willing to divide one of those dollars into ten dimes and give a dime to every panhandler you can who asks you for money? Or divide ten dollars of your hundred for the week into ten singles to give one dollar for everyone who asks you for money? Or divide one hundred dollars of your one thousand dollars into twenty five-dollar bills to give five dollars to everyone who asks you for money? Getting the picture?

Will there be times when it isn't feasible to give what people ask of us? Yes, but that doesn't excuse us from still trying to help. You wouldn't give a stick of dynamite a match, nor would you give an addict the resources to feed his or her habit. However, we shouldn't use a person's condition as an excuse to not do anything for them.

This way of giving can apply to all areas of our lives whether it is with our resources, time, or ourselves. You see, our giving is not based primarily on the amount we give but the spirit in which we give. The focus is to develop a spirit of comfort in giving and one of discomfort when we don't, rather than the customary feeling of discomfort for many of us in our giving. Along with our giving, I believe one of the greatest gifts we can give is the gift of hope. And one of the greatest hopes we can offer to someone in our giving is that someone cares.

What about those who steal for a living? However subtle or harmless you may consider your hustle to receive access to someone's kindness, whatever you receive from them, if it is done by deceit, is no different than stealing. Paul spoke on this in his letter to the

Ephesian church (Ephesians 4:28). This scripture encompasses all who acquire unjust gain whether by trickery, force, or any other means because they refuse to labor for a living. Paul tells them to stop stealing and work so they can assist those who truly are in need.

A thief is a thief—even those who freeload off the generosity of others. Choosing a life of freeloading and swindling for a living rather than earning it is nothing short of stealing from those who are generous and from those who truly had need of what you refuse to work for. Stop it! Strive to earn your living so you can be a benefit to those truly in need.

We are one another's keeper. Iron sharpening iron. Encouraging each other and edifying the Body of Christ. When we help someone, we should do so with the mind-set that God is blessing us to be a blessing and not that we are the ones doing the blessing. Humility teaches that it's not how proud we should feel after performing acts of kindness but how grateful.

One thing I am learning with every opportunity God gives me to share is that what God shares with me is not just for me. But I should share some of it to benefit as many people as possible, whether they're in the Body of Christ or not.

Finally, in our walk with God, we should always keep a servant's heart. Whatever our maturity level may be, or whatever position of authority we may hold within the Body of Christ, we should never stop being servants of God. How we served earlier in our salvation may not be the same as to how we serve now, but we should still have a desire to serve.

In the early years of the New Testament church, the apostles told members of the church that it was not for them to leave what they were doing to address their issues (Acts 6:2). Not to stop serving but to be able to serve more freely in their ministry.

If anything, as we grow more mature in Christ and as God elevates us to positions of authority and responsibility, the more accountable we should feel in our service to God and one another (Luke 12:47–48). Know that with greater understanding comes greater responsibility, and those with greater responsibility are required that much more to serve as a leader leading by example (Luke 22:24–27).

Paul understood the importance of being an example of serving even though he knew he was in position to demand more from those he served and served with. But he chose to lighten their burden by working along with them so that he could contribute rather than being served (2 Thessalonians 3:6–15). Am I saying that we should not honor our leaders and shepherds of God in service? No, but we should not use our position or authority in Christ to excuse us from being of service to others.

There's always an opportunity for us to serve through our sharing and giving regardless of our position in Christ. We're all cultivators in God's vineyard, which spans far beyond the walls of a church building and reaches out wherever there is a need to minister to lost and troubled souls. We need to start reaching out to those in need to become the true leader God is calling us out to be. Whether it is with our finances, time, or person, we all must strive to do good when the occasion arises: "But do not forget to do good and to share, for with such sacrifices God is well pleased" (Hebrews 13:16 NKJV). God bless you all, with the love of Jesus Christ, Bro. Tariek.

About the Author

Tariek is a licensed and ordained minister and considers himself to be a vineyard shepherd. In his thirty-five years of salvation he has served as a Sunday School Teacher, Church Youth Director, Director of Ministry to the Illinois Department of Corrections Juvenile Division, and Pastor. He has also served in ministries involving the homeless, Seniors at Nursing Homes, Adult Correctional facilities, and numerous Street Ministries to proclaim the Gospel of Jesus Christ. In his book he speaks on "Servanthood as a call and avenue to glorify God", supporting his personal passion and belief with God's Word.

Printed in the United States
by Baker & Taylor Publisher Services